ACT TODAY

*Daily Act Practices To Unhook
From Your Struggles, And Live
Your Rich & Meaningful Life*

Bill Stevens

RedChair

Copyright © 2024 Bill Stevens

All rights reserved

Disclaimer

The information and suggestions provided in this publication are for educational purposes only. The reader is advised to take full responsibility for their own health and well-being when applying any advice, exercises, or suggestions from this book. While Acceptance and Commitment Therapy (ACT) can be a useful approach in addressing various mental health conditions, this book is not intended to replace professional therapy or medical treatment.

In the event of serious or ongoing issues related to any of the conditions targeted in this publication (including, but not limited to, addiction, ADHD, anxiety, anger, apathy, and stress), readers are strongly encouraged to seek guidance from licensed healthcare providers, mental health professionals, or other appropriate medical services. This book should not be considered a substitute for professional help, especially in times of crisis.

Bill Stevens, as the author, and Red Chair Therapy (redchair.co.uk), as the publisher, take no responsibility for any decisions, actions, or outcomes that may result from applying the material in this publication. Readers are encouraged to use the insights and exercises in conjunction with professional therapy or support.

Copyright for any referenced or public domain material has been acknowledged where applicable, and all rights remain with the original authors. Special thanks to the ACT community, researchers, and providers of public information who have contributed to the growth and development of Acceptance and Commitment Therapy. We also wish to acknowledge the role of AI in helping to compile and organise this publication

No part of this book may be reproduced, or stored in a retrieval system, or transmitted in any form or by any means, electronic, mechanical, photocopying, recording, or otherwise, without express written permission of the publisher.

ISBN: 9798340659910

Cover design by: Bill Stevens
Library of Congress Control Number: 2018675309
Printed in the United States of America

Dedicated to my wife Janet, where words are not enough. Everyone needs a super angel in thier lives.

CONTENTS

Title Page
Copyright
Dedication
Introduction
January	1
February	33
March	63
April	95
May	126
June	158
July	189
August	221
September	253
October	284
November	316
December	348
Conditions and Struggles	380
Acceptance and Commitment Therapy (ACT)	389

Acknowledgement	397
About The Author	399

INTRODUCTION
Welcome to ACT Today

by Bill Stevens - ACT Therapist

Every morning, the struggles we face—whether it's addiction, anxiety, anger, ADHD, stress, or anything else—seem to sit at the end of the bed, waiting for us to wake up, saying, "I'm glad you're awake, I've got work for you." This is really our own fusion with unhelpful thoughts, the ones that initiate the struggle and keep us stuck.

With thousands of hours of experience working with clients, I've noticed something: those who benefit the most from therapy often find real value in building a daily habit and a fresh perspective. ACT Today was compiled specifically as a companion to Acceptance and Commitment Therapy because my clients needed something practical, something they could use every day to stay focused on their values and committed action.

By picking up this book first thing in the morning and reading a short entry, you're choosing a values-based action. It's a simple but powerful step that helps interrupt old habits and keeps you grounded. You don't need to fix everything all at once—just focus on today.

Focusing on just one day at a time is a proven way to create lasting, effective change. Let ACT Toda be your guide, helping you pause, reflect, and take meaningful action, one step at a time

Bill Stevens

JANUARY

January 1

Quote

"The best way out is always through." – *Robert Frost*

Insight

Acceptance means fully experiencing the present moment, even when it's painful. Avoiding discomfort only prolongs it, while moving through it allows us to grow.

Task

Reflect on a recent challenge. How did avoidance or resistance affect it? Today, practice acceptance by allowing any discomfort to be present without fighting it.

Metaphor

The Chinese Finger Trap – When you try to pull your fingers out of the trap, it tightens. The way out is to move into the trap, loosening it. Similarly, moving into discomfort can release its grip on us.

January 2

Quote

"Life is 10% what happens to us and 90% how we react to it." – *Charles R. Swindoll*

Insight

Self-as-context allows us to see that we are not our thoughts or feelings. We are the observers, the space in which experiences happen, and we can choose how to respond.

Task

When a strong thought or feeling arises today, take a moment to notice it without judgement. Remind yourself, "I am not my thoughts or emotions; I am the observer."

Metaphor

The Chessboard – Your thoughts and feelings are like pieces on a chessboard. They move, but you are the board itself—steady, solid, and unmoving, no matter what happens in the game.

January 3

Quote

"Between stimulus and response, there is a space. In that space is our power to choose our response." – *Viktor Frankl*

Insight

Present moment awareness gives us the space to choose how to respond instead of reacting on autopilot. That small pause can make all the difference.

Task

Throughout the day, practice noticing when you're on autopilot. Pause before responding and ask, "What response would be most aligned with my values?"

Metaphor

Dropping Anchor – In the middle of a storm, a ship drops anchor to stay grounded. In the same way, present moment awareness anchors you when emotions and thoughts swirl around.

January 4

Quote

"It's not what you look at that matters, it's what you see." – *Henry David Thoreau*

Insight

Defusion helps us see thoughts for what they are—just thoughts, not reality. By stepping back from our thoughts, we gain perspective and can choose how to act.

Task

When you notice an unhelpful thought today, try saying, "I'm having the thought that…" and see how it shifts your perspective.

Metaphor

The Leaves on a Stream – Imagine your thoughts as leaves floating down a stream. You don't have to grab onto them; just watch them float by.

January 5: Stress

Quote

"The greatest weapon against stress is our ability to choose one thought over another." – *William James*

Insight

Stress often arises from the stories we tell ourselves about what's happening. Defusion helps us separate from those stories and see things more clearly.

Task

Next time you feel stressed today, pause and ask yourself, "Is this a thought or a fact?" Notice how your relationship to the stress shifts when you see it as a thought.

Metaphor

The Thought Train – Thoughts are like trains passing by. You don't have to hop on every one. You can stand on the platform and watch them go by without getting on board.

January 6: ADHD

Quote

"Concentrate all your thoughts upon the work at hand. The sun's rays do not burn until brought to a focus." – *Alexander Graham Bell*

Insight

ADHD makes it challenging to focus, but through acceptance, we can stop battling with our minds and instead create structures that support focus.

Task

Today, try breaking a task into small, manageable chunks. Set a timer for 10 minutes and focus on just one chunk without multitasking.

Metaphor

Focusing the Sunlight – Imagine your attention is like sunlight. When it's scattered, it warms, but when focused, it can start a fire.

January 7

Quote

"We must be willing to let go of the life we planned so as to have the life that is waiting for us." *–Joseph Campbell*

Insight

Acceptance isn't about giving up, but about letting go of our struggle against reality. By accepting what is, we create space for new possibilities to emerge.

Task

Identify one area in your life where you're struggling against reality. Today, practice accepting it as it is, without judgement, and notice what possibilities arise.

Metaphor

The Tug-of-War with the Monster – Imagine you're in a tug-of-war with a monster, pulling on the rope. What happens if you drop the rope? Acceptance is like dropping the rope, freeing up your energy.

January 8

Quote

"Happiness is not something ready made. It comes from your own actions." – *Dalai Lama*

Insight

Committed action in ACT is about taking steps toward what matters, even when it's hard. We create happiness not by waiting for it, but by living in alignment with our values.

Task

Identify one small action today that aligns with your values. Take that action, even if it feels difficult or uncomfortable.

Metaphor

The Path – Committed action is like walking down a path. Each step may feel small, but with persistence, those steps take you closer to a meaningful life.

January 9

Quote

"To be yourself in a world that is constantly trying to make you something else is the greatest accomplishment." – *Ralph Waldo Emerson*

Insight

Self-as-context teaches that you are more than your thoughts, emotions, or the labels others put on you. You are the observer of all these experiences, and that's where your true self lies.

Task

Take five minutes today to sit quietly and observe your thoughts. Remind yourself that you are not your thoughts; you are the one observing them.

Metaphor

The Sky and the Weather – You are like the sky, vast and unchanging. Your thoughts and emotions are like the weather, constantly shifting but never affecting the sky itself.

January 10: Addiction

Quote

"The only way to make sense out of change is to plunge into it, move with it, and join the dance." – *Alan Watts*

Insight

Recovery from addiction involves accepting change and uncertainty. By staying present and committed to your values, you can navigate the ups and downs of recovery.

Task

When cravings arise today, notice them without judgement. Take three deep breaths, and reconnect with a value that motivates your recovery.

Metaphor

The Stormy Seas – Recovery is like navigating stormy seas. The waves may be rough, but your values are like a compass, guiding you through the storm.

January 11

Quote

"The only person you are destined to become is the person you decide to be." – *Ralph Waldo Emerson*

Insight

Values give us direction, but it's up to us to take the steps toward becoming the person we want to be. Each small action we take moves us closer to that vision.

Task

Identify one of your core values and write down one small action you can take today to live in alignment with that value.

Metaphor

The Compass and the Journey – Values are like a compass. They give you direction, but it's up to you to take the steps along the journey.

January 12

Quote

"It's never too late to be what you might have been." – *George Eliot*

Insight

Acceptance means letting go of regret about the past. It's never too late to take committed action toward a meaningful life, no matter where you are now.

Task

Identify one regret you've been holding onto. Today, practice accepting it, and write down one step you can take to move forward.

Metaphor

The Garden of Your Life – Imagine your life as a garden. You can't change what was planted in the past, but you can always start planting new seeds today.

January 13

Quote

"Do not dwell in the past, do not dream of the future, concentrate the mind on the present moment." – *Buddha*

Insight

Present moment awareness allows us to fully experience life as it unfolds. By staying present, we free ourselves from the regrets of the past and the anxieties of the future.

Task

Take five minutes today to engage in mindful breathing. Notice the sensations of each breath, and when your mind wanders, gently bring it back to the present moment.

Metaphor

The Anchor – The present moment is like an anchor that keeps you grounded amidst the waves of past and future concerns.

January 14: Stress

Quote

"It's not the load that breaks you down, it's the way you carry it." – *Lena Horne*

Insight

Stress is often about how we relate to challenges. Acceptance allows us to carry our load in a way that's more manageable, by letting go of the struggle.

Task

Next time something unexpected happens today, pause for a moment. Notice your automatic reaction, and then choose a response based on your values.

Metaphor

The Space Between Stimulus and Response – Imagine a pause button between what happens and how you react. Acceptance gives you the space to press pause and choose a meaningful response.

January 15

Quote

"Holding on to anger is like drinking poison and expecting the other person to die." – *Buddha*

Insight

Anger is a natural emotion, but holding on to it causes suffering. Acceptance helps us experience anger without letting it control us.

Task

When anger arises today, take three deep breaths. Notice how it feels in your body, and see if you can allow it to be there without acting on it.

Metaphor

The Hot Coal – Anger is like holding a hot coal, hoping to throw it at someone else. The longer you hold it, the more you burn yourself.

January 16

Quote

"There is no greater agony than bearing an untold story inside you." – *Maya Angelou*

Insight

Acceptance helps us face difficult truths about ourselves and our experiences. Sharing your story, even with yourself, creates space for healing.

Task

Spend five minutes today writing down a part of your story that you've been avoiding. Notice any feelings that come up, and see if you can allow them to be present.

Metaphor

The Balloon – Difficult emotions are like balloons we hold inside. When we express them, we release the pressure and let them float away.

January 17: Stress

Quote

"Worry never robs tomorrow of its sorrow, it only saps today of its joy." – *Leo Buscaglia*

Insight

Stress about the future drains our energy in the present. Acceptance allows us to stay grounded in today, even when future concerns are present.

Task

Next time you notice a worry today, ask yourself, "Is this something I can control right now?" If not, gently let it go and return your focus to the present.

Metaphor

The Present as a Gift – The present moment is like an unopened gift. When we focus on future worries, we leave today's gifts unopened.

January 18: Growth

Quote

"What we fear of doing most is usually what we most need to do." – *Ralph Waldo Emerson*

Insight

Growth often happens when we step out of our comfort zone. Committed action means facing fear and discomfort in the pursuit of meaningful goals.

Task

Identify one area in your life where fear is holding you back. What is one small step you can take today to move in the direction of growth?

Metaphor

The Comfort Zone – Growth is like a plant pushing through the soil. It takes effort and discomfort, but it's necessary for reaching the light.

January 19

Quote

"The only journey is the one within." – *Rainer Maria Rilke*

Insight

Self-as-context reminds us that no matter what happens externally, we can always turn inward and find the observer within. You are the constant in your ever-changing experiences.

Task

Spend five minutes today sitting in silence. Notice your thoughts and feelings, but don't engage with them. Instead, observe them, knowing you are the space in which they appear.

Metaphor

The Sky and the Clouds – Imagine your mind as the sky, and your thoughts and feelings as clouds. The sky remains vast and unchanged, even as the clouds pass by.

January 20

Quote

"Do not go where the path may lead, go instead where there is no path and leave a trail." – *Ralph Waldo Emerson*

Insight

Committed action involves creating your own path based on your values, rather than following the one laid out by others. Your journey is unique, and it's shaped by the choices you make.

Task

Identify one small action today that aligns with a value of yours, even if it's different from what others expect. Take that action and notice how it feels to walk your own path.

Metaphor

Blazing Your Trail – Committed action is like walking through a forest without a path. Every step creates a new path, and you move forward guided by your inner compass—your values.

January 21: Anger

Quote

"Speak when you are angry and you will make the best speech you will ever regret." – *Ambrose Bierce*

Insight

Anger can cloud your judgement and lead to actions we regret. Through defusion and acceptance, we can experience anger without letting it control our behaviour.

Task

Next time you feel anger rising today, take a moment to pause and breathe. Label the emotion: "I am having the feeling of anger," and see if this creates some space between you and the emotion.

Metaphor

The Volcano – Anger is like a volcano, building pressure. When you notice it, rather than letting it erupt, you can release some steam by breathing and acknowledging the feeling.

January 22

Quote

"Life isn't about finding yourself. Life is about creating yourself." – *George Bernard Shaw*

Insight

Values give us the blueprint for the person we want to become. Through committed action, we create ourselves each day by choosing actions aligned with our deepest values.

Task

Identify one of your values and write down one thing you can do today to embody that value. Take action, knowing that each step you take is part of creating yourself.

Metaphor

The Sculptor – Imagine you are a sculptor and your life is the sculpture. Every action you take is like a chisel stroke, shaping the person you are becoming.

January 23

Quote

"Change the way you look at things, and the things you look at change." – *Wayne Dyer*

Insight

Defusion helps us change our perspective on thoughts and emotions. By seeing them as temporary and not identifying with them, we can change the way we relate to them.

Task

When you notice a difficult thought today, practice saying, "I'm having the thought that…" and see if this small shift helps you see the thought in a different way.

Metaphor

The Fish in Water – We are often so immersed in our thoughts that we don't even notice them. Defusion is like stepping out of the water and seeing the thoughts for what they are—just thoughts.

January 24: Apathy

Quote

"In any given moment, we have two options: to step forward into growth or to step back into safety." – *Abraham Maslow*

Insight

Apathy often comes from fear or uncertainty. Committed action asks us to take steps forward, even when we feel stuck or unsure. Moving toward our values helps break the cycle of inaction.

Task

Think of an area where you've felt apathetic recently. What is one small action you can take today to move forward, even if it's a tiny step? Take that step and notice how it feels.

Metaphor

The Stuck Car – Apathy is like a car stuck in the mud. It feels easier not to move, but taking small actions is like pushing the car little by little until it gets unstuck.

January 25

Quote

"Success is not the key to happiness. Happiness is the key to success. If you love what you are doing, you will be successful." – *Albert Schweitzer*

Insight

Living in alignment with your values creates a sense of fulfilment, which is the foundation of true success. Committed action grounded in values leads to a rich and meaningful life.

Task

Reflect on your current goals. How do they align with your values? If they don't, consider one small change you could make to bring them into better alignment.

Metaphor

The Fulfilment Compass – Imagine that values are like a compass guiding you toward fulfilment. When your actions align with your values, you are moving in the direction of success.

January 26

Quote

"You cannot swim for new horizons until you have courage to lose sight of the shore." – *William Faulkner*

Insight

Growth often requires stepping into uncertainty. By accepting the unknown and committing to action, we open ourselves up to new possibilities and experiences.

Task

Identify one area in your life where you've been holding back due to fear of the unknown. Today, take one small step in that area, trusting that growth lies beyond your comfort zone.

Metaphor

The Leap of Faith – Growth is like jumping off a cliff into water. You won't know what's beneath until you take the leap, but the courage to jump opens up new horizons.

January 27

Quote

"We don't see things as they are, we see them as we are."
– *Anaïs Nin*

Insight

Present moment awareness allows us to step back from our assumptions and see the world as it is, not filtered through our biases and expectations. This creates space for new understanding.

Task

Today, practice noticing the thoughts or assumptions you bring to situations. See if you can let them go and approach each moment with curiosity and openness.

Metaphor

The Foggy Glasses – Imagine you're wearing glasses smudged with fog. Your assumptions are like that fog, clouding your view. Present moment awareness is like wiping the glasses clean, allowing you to see more clearly.

January 28: Anger

Quote

"Holding on to anger is like drinking poison and expecting the other person to die." – *Buddha*

Insight

Anger is a natural emotion, but holding on to it causes suffering. Acceptance helps us experience anger without letting it control us.

Task

When anger arises today, take three deep breaths. Notice how it feels in your body, and see if you can allow it to be there without acting on it.

Metaphor

The Hot Coal – Anger is like holding a hot coal, hoping to throw it at someone else. The longer you hold it, the more you burn yourself.

January 29

Quote

"Life is what happens when you're busy making other plans." – *John Lennon*

Insight

Present moment awareness helps us embrace the unpredictability of life. By staying open to what's happening right now, we can find joy and meaning in the here and now, even when things don't go according to plan.

Task

Today, practice being present with the unexpected. Notice if something doesn't go the way you planned, and see if you can embrace the moment as it is, rather than resisting it.

Metaphor

The River – Life is like a river. You can't control its flow, but you can choose to go with the current or struggle against it. Present moment awareness helps you flow with life's twists and turns.

January 30

Quote

"Success is not final, failure is not fatal: it is the courage to continue that counts." – *Winston Churchill*

Insight

Success and failure are just points on the journey. What truly matters is your willingness to keep moving forward, guided by your values. Committed action means staying the course, no matter the outcome.

Task

Reflect on a recent failure or setback. What value can you reconnect with today to keep moving forward? Write it down and take one small step in alignment with that value.

Metaphor

The Long Road – Success is like walking down a long road. There will be bumps and detours, but as long as you keep moving, guided by your values, you are on the right path.

January 31: ADHD

Quote

"The mind is everything. What you think you become."
— *Buddha*

Insight

With ADHD, thoughts can feel scattered or overwhelming. Defusion helps you step back from your thoughts, seeing them for what they are—just thoughts, not facts. This can create more space to act intentionally.

Task

Today, when your mind feels scattered, practice defusion. Label each thought as "just a thought," and bring your focus back to the task at hand, one step at a time.

Metaphor

The Traffic Jam – Imagine your mind as a busy highway, full of thoughts like cars speeding by. Defusion is like stepping off the highway and watching the cars pass by, without needing to jump in.

FEBRUARY

February 1

Quote

"You are what you do, not what you say you'll do." – *C.G. Jung*

Insight

Committed action involves doing what matters to you, not just thinking or talking about it. Living in alignment with your values requires consistent, value-based action.

Task

Identify one value you hold dear, and take one small action today that moves you toward living that value more fully.

Metaphor

The Builder – Imagine your life as a house you're building. Each action you take is like a brick being placed in that house. The more you act in line with your values, the stronger your foundation becomes.

February 2

Quote

"Happiness is not something ready made. It comes from your own actions." – *Dalai Lama*

Insight

Happiness comes from living a life aligned with your values. By taking committed action and living in line with what truly matters to you, you create a meaningful and fulfilling life.

Task

Take five minutes today to reflect on what brings you genuine happiness. How can you take action today to align your life with those values?

Metaphor

Planting Seeds – Happiness is like a garden. You have to plant seeds, water them, and tend to them over time. The actions you take are the seeds you plant for a fulfilling life.

February 3

Quote

"You can't stop the waves, but you can learn to surf." – *Jon Kabat-Zinn*

Insight

Acceptance means allowing life to unfold without fighting against it. Challenges are inevitable, but with acceptance, you can learn to navigate them with greater ease.

Task

Identify a situation in your life that you've been resisting. Practice accepting it today, even if it's difficult. Notice how this shift affects your experience.

Metaphor

The Ocean – Life is like the ocean, full of waves. You can't stop the waves from coming, but by accepting them, you can learn to ride them instead of being overwhelmed.

February 4

Quote

"Don't watch the clock; do what it does. Keep going." – *Sam Levenson*

Insight

Committed action means moving forward even when progress feels slow or difficult. The key is to keep taking steps in the direction of your values, no matter how small.

Task

Identify one task today that you've been putting off. Break it down into a small step, and commit to taking action on it today, regardless of the outcome.

Metaphor

The Marathon – Life is like a marathon, not a sprint. Progress comes from consistent effort over time, not from rushing or forcing results.

February 5: ADHD

Quote

"Focus on the journey, not the destination. Joy is found not in finishing an activity but in doing it." – *Greg Anderson*

Insight

For those with ADHD, staying present with a task can be challenging. Present moment awareness helps you focus on the process, rather than getting overwhelmed by the end goal.

Task

Pick a task today and set a timer for five minutes. During that time, focus only on the task at hand. When your mind wanders, gently bring it back to the present moment.

Metaphor

The Spotlight – Your attention is like a spotlight. You can only shine it on one thing at a time. Present moment awareness helps you focus your spotlight where it matters.

February 6

Quote

"The only way to make sense out of change is to plunge into it, move with it, and join the dance." – *Alan Watts*

Insight

Change is inevitable, and resisting it only causes suffering. Acceptance allows us to move with change, rather than fighting against it, leading to a more fluid and adaptive life.

Task

Reflect on a recent change in your life. How have you been resisting it? Today, practice accepting that change and see how this shift affects your perspective.

Metaphor

The Dance – Life is like a dance. The more you resist the rhythm, the harder it becomes. Acceptance is like learning to move with the music, allowing you to flow with life's changes.

February 7: Anger

Quote

"For every minute you are angry you lose sixty seconds of happiness." – *Ralph Waldo Emerson*

Insight

Anger can consume our attention and keep us from living fully. Acceptance allows us to experience anger without getting lost in it, creating space for other emotions.

Task

Next time you feel anger today, pause for a moment. Acknowledge the feeling without judgement, and practice letting it pass without reacting to it.

Metaphor

The Storm – Anger is like a storm. It can feel overwhelming, but it always passes. The more we can accept the storm, the easier it becomes to weather it.

February 8

Quote

"You miss 100% of the shots you don't take." – *Wayne Gretzky*

Insight

Committed action means taking risks and stepping out of your comfort zone. By avoiding action, you miss the chance for growth and new experiences.

Task

Identify one area in your life where you've been holding back. Take one small step today toward that area, knowing that even small actions matter.

Metaphor

The Door – Growth is like a door. Every action you take is like a key that unlocks new possibilities. By taking action, you open new doors to growth and opportunity.

February 9

Quote

"In the middle of every difficulty lies opportunity." – *Albert Einstein*

Insight

Defusion helps us see past our immediate thoughts and emotions, allowing us to find opportunities in difficult situations. By stepping back from our thoughts, we can see new possibilities.

Task

Next time you face a challenge today, take a moment to step back from your thoughts. Ask yourself, "What opportunity might be hiding in this situation?"

Metaphor

The Silver Lining – Difficulties are like clouds. Sometimes, you need to step back to see the silver lining behind them. Defusion helps you find the hidden opportunities in challenges.

February 10: Addiction

Quote

"Recovery is not for people who need it, it's for people who want it." – *Anonymous*

Insight

Overcoming addiction requires a commitment to value-based action. It's not enough to want change intellectually—you have to be willing to take consistent steps toward recovery, even when it's difficult.

Task

Reflect on your journey toward recovery. Identify one small, value-based action you can take today to support your recovery, and commit to it fully.

Metaphor

The Ladder – Recovery is like climbing a ladder. Every step, no matter how small, brings you closer to the top. Committed action means taking one step at a time, even when the climb feels steep.

February 11

Quote

"The best way to predict the future is to create it." – *Abraham Lincoln*

Insight

Committed action allows you to shape your future. By consistently taking value-driven steps, you actively create the life you want to live, rather than waiting for it to happen.

Task

Choose one aspect of your future that matters to you. Identify a small step you can take today to bring that future closer, and commit to taking it.

Metaphor

The Sculptor – Imagine your life as a block of stone. Every action you take is like a chisel stroke, slowly shaping the sculpture of your future. Through consistent action, you create the masterpiece of your life.

February 12

Quote

"The present moment is filled with joy and happiness. If you are attentive, you will see it." – *Thich Nhat Hanh*

Insight

The present moment is the only time we truly have. By staying fully present, we open ourselves to the joy and richness available in each moment, regardless of external circumstances.

Task

Take five minutes today to pause and breathe. Notice what is happening around you and within you, without trying to change anything. Just be present with whatever is.

Metaphor

The Sunrise – Life is like a sunrise. If you're too busy rushing around, you might miss it. Present moment awareness allows you to stop and appreciate the beauty in each moment.

February 13

Quote

"Do not dwell in the past, do not dream of the future, concentrate the mind on the present moment." – *Buddha*

Insight

Present moment awareness allows you to fully engage with life as it happens. When we get caught up in the past or future, we miss out on the richness of the present.

Task

Whenever you notice your mind drifting to the past or future today, gently bring it back to the present. Focus on what you can see, hear, and feel in this moment.

Metaphor

The Time Traveller – Your mind is like a time traveller, constantly moving between the past and the future. Present moment awareness is like bringing it back to the here and now, where life is actually happening.

February 14

Quote

"Love and compassion are necessities, not luxuries. Without them, humanity cannot survive." – *Dalai Lama*

Insight

Compassion is an essential value in living a meaningful life. By acting with kindness toward yourself and others, you create deeper connections and contribute to a more compassionate world.

Task

Perform one act of kindness today, either for yourself or for someone else. Notice how this small action impacts your sense of connection and meaning.

Metaphor

The Ripple – Acts of compassion are like dropping a stone into a pond. Each kind action creates ripples that spread out and touch others, contributing to a more compassionate world.

February 15

Quote

"When we are no longer able to change a situation, we are challenged to change ourselves." – *Viktor Frankl*

Insight

Acceptance means recognising that some things are beyond our control. By focusing on what you can change—your actions and attitude—you free yourself from unnecessary suffering.

Task

Identify one situation in your life that you cannot change. Practice accepting it fully today, and shift your focus to what you can control: your response to it.

Metaphor

The Weather – Life is like the weather. You can't control the rain, but you can choose whether to carry an umbrella. Acceptance helps you focus on what you can control, rather than fighting what you cannot.

February 16: Apathy

Quote

"The price of apathy towards public affairs is to be ruled by evil men." – *Plato*

Insight

Apathy often stems from feeling overwhelmed or disconnected. By reconnecting with your values and taking small, meaningful actions, you can break free from the paralysis of apathy.

Task

Identify one area of your life where you've been feeling apathetic. Take one small step today toward re-engaging with that area, no matter how small the action.

Metaphor

The Frozen Lake – Apathy is like a frozen lake. Beneath the ice, life is still there, waiting to break free. Value-based action is like the warmth that melts the ice, allowing life to flow again.

February 17

Quote

"He who has a why to live for can bear almost any how."
– *Friedrich Nietzsche*

Insight

Your values provide the "why" for your life. When you're clear on what matters most to you, you can endure challenges with greater resilience and purpose.

Task

Reflect on your core values today. Write down one of your values and consider how it can guide your actions, especially during difficult times.

Metaphor

The Compass – Values are like a compass, always pointing you in the direction of your true north. When you follow your values, you have a clear sense of direction, even in the face of adversity.

February 18

Quote

"Your present circumstances don't determine where you can go; they merely determine where you start." – *Nido Qubein*

Insight

Defusion allows you to see your thoughts as temporary and not definitive. You can choose to act in alignment with your values, no matter what your thoughts say.

Task

Whenever a negative thought arises today, remind yourself: "This is just a thought, not a fact." Practice defusing from that thought and returning to the present.

Metaphor

The Cloud – Your thoughts are like clouds passing through the sky. Defusion helps you step back and observe them, rather than getting caught in the storm they might create.

February 19: Stress

Quote

"Do not anticipate trouble, or worry about what may never happen. Keep in the sunlight." – *Benjamin Franklin*

Insight

Stress often comes from worrying about the future. Present moment awareness helps you stay grounded in the here and now, rather than getting lost in what might happen.

Task

When you feel stressed today, pause and take three deep breaths. Focus on the sensations in your body and bring your attention back to the present moment.

Metaphor

The Anchor – Present moment awareness is like an anchor in a storm. When stress pulls you in different directions, you can use your breath and body to ground yourself in the present moment.

February 20

Quote

"Our greatest glory is not in never falling, but in rising every time we fall." – *Confucius*

Insight

Committed action is not about avoiding failure—it's about getting back up when you fall. Resilience comes from continuing to take action, even when things don't go as planned.

Task

Think of a recent setback or failure. How can you take one step today to move forward, even if it's a small one? Commit to taking that step.

Metaphor

The Phoenix – Resilience is like the phoenix, rising from the ashes. Each time you get back up and take action, you rise stronger than before.

February 21

Quote

"Believe you can and you're halfway there." – *Theodore Roosevelt*

Insight

Self-as-context helps you see yourself as more than your thoughts and feelings. When you believe in your ability to take action, you create the space to move toward your values, regardless of self-doubt.

Task

Identify one limiting belief that has been holding you back. Today, take a small action that challenges that belief, even if it's uncomfortable.

Metaphor

The Observer – Imagine yourself as an observer, watching your thoughts and feelings from a distance. By seeing yourself as more than your thoughts, you create space for new possibilities.

February 22: ADHD

Quote

"The mind is like a parachute. It doesn't work unless it's open." – *Frank Zappa*

Insight

For people with ADHD, it's easy to get stuck in patterns of distraction or overwhelm. Defusion helps by creating space between you and your thoughts, allowing for greater focus and flexibility.

Task

Next time your mind starts to wander today, pause and notice your thoughts. Practice defusion by telling yourself, "I'm noticing that my mind is distracted," and then gently bring your attention back to the task at hand.

Metaphor

The Thought Train – Your thoughts are like trains passing through a station. You don't have to get on every train that arrives. Defusion helps you watch the trains go by without getting carried away.

February 23

Quote

"The secret of getting ahead is getting started." – *Mark Twain*

Insight

Committed action begins with taking that first step. Even if it's small, starting creates momentum that can carry you forward toward your values.

Task

Identify one task today that you've been procrastinating on. Break it down into the smallest possible step, and commit to taking action on that step today.

Metaphor

The First Step – Life is like a long journey, and every journey starts with a single step. By taking that first step, you set the direction for the rest of your journey.

February 24: Addiction

Quote

"The only way out is through." – *Robert Frost*

Insight

Overcoming addiction requires facing the discomfort of withdrawal and cravings. Acceptance allows you to experience that discomfort without giving in to it, knowing that it will eventually pass.

Task

Next time you experience a craving or urge today, pause and take three deep breaths. Practice accepting the discomfort without acting on it, and notice how it changes over time.

Metaphor

The Tunnel – Addiction recovery is like going through a tunnel. It's dark and uncomfortable, but if you keep moving forward, you'll eventually come out the other side into the light.

February 25

Quote

"It is not the mountain we conquer, but ourselves." – *Sir Edmund Hillary*

Insight

Self-as-context allows you to see that the biggest challenges in life are not external, but internal. By understanding and accepting yourself, you can navigate life's challenges with greater clarity and purpose.

Task

Take a few minutes today to reflect on an internal challenge you've been facing. How can you approach it with acceptance and self-compassion?

Metaphor

The Mirror – Life's challenges are like looking into a mirror. They reflect back aspects of ourselves that we need to understand and accept in order to grow.

February 26: Anger

Quote

"Holding onto anger is like drinking poison and expecting the other person to die." – *Buddha*

Insight

Anger, when held onto, only harms ourselves. Acceptance allows us to acknowledge our anger without letting it consume us, creating space for other emotions to arise.

Task

Next time you feel anger today, pause and notice the physical sensations in your body. Practice accepting those sensations without reacting to them, and notice how your experience changes.

Metaphor

The Hot Coal – Anger is like holding onto a hot coal. The longer you hold it, the more it burns you. By accepting anger and letting it go, you free yourself from its pain.

February 27

Quote

"Success is not final, failure is not fatal: it is the courage to continue that counts." – *Winston Churchill*

Insight

Growth comes from persistence, not perfection. Whether you succeed or fail, what matters most is that you keep taking committed action toward your values, no matter the outcome.

Task

Reflect on a recent success or failure. How can you continue moving forward, regardless of the result? Take one step today that aligns with your values.

Metaphor

The Climb – Life is like climbing a mountain. Success and failure are just steps along the way. What matters is that you keep climbing, even when the path is difficult.

February 28

Quote

"A year from now you may wish you had started today."
– Karen Lamb

Insight

Procrastination often stems from fear or avoidance. Committed action means starting now, even if it's uncomfortable, because every step you take today brings you closer to your goals.

Task

Identify one goal you've been putting off. Take one small action today to start working toward that goal, no matter how small the step.

Metaphor

The Garden – Your life is like a garden. Every action you take is like planting a seed. By starting today, you begin to cultivate the life you want to grow in the future.

February 29 (Leap Year)

Quote

"Time is what we want most, but what we use worst." – *William Penn*

Insight

Time is a precious resource, and how we spend it determines the quality of our lives. By living in alignment with your values, you ensure that you use your time in a way that feels meaningful and fulfilling.

Task

Reflect on how you've spent your time recently. Are you living in line with your values? Identify one area where you can better align your time with what matters most to you, and take action today.

Metaphor

The Hourglass – Time is like an hourglass, and the sand is always falling. Each moment is precious, and by living in line with your values, you make the most of the time you have.

MARCH

March 1

Quote

"The journey of a thousand miles begins with one step."
– *Lao Tzu*

Insight

Every big goal is achieved through a series of small steps. Committed action is about breaking things down into manageable steps and moving forward, no matter how small.

Task

Identify one task or goal that feels overwhelming. Break it down into its smallest possible step, and take that step today.

Metaphor

The Bricklayer – Building a wall is overwhelming if you think of it as a whole. But if you lay one brick at a time, with care, eventually you'll have a strong wall.

March 2

Quote

"Happiness is not something ready-made. It comes from your own actions." – *Dalai Lama*

Insight

Living a rich and meaningful life doesn't happen by chance. It's cultivated by taking action that aligns with your values, even when it's difficult or uncomfortable.

Task

Reflect on what makes life meaningful to you. Take one action today that helps you create a richer and more fulfilling life, no matter how small.

Metaphor

The Garden – A meaningful life is like a garden. It requires regular attention, care, and action. By planting seeds and nurturing them, you create a flourishing life over time.

March 3

Quote

"In three words I can sum up everything I've learned about life: It goes on." – *Robert Frost*

Insight

Acceptance means allowing life to be as it is, without needing to change or control everything. Things will keep moving, and your task is to flow with life rather than resist it.

Task

Identify one thing today that is bothering you. Practice accepting it fully without needing to change or resist it. Notice how this shift affects your emotional state.

Metaphor

The River – Life is like a river, constantly flowing. By accepting the current rather than fighting it, you find greater ease and peace along the way.

March 4

Quote

"What lies behind us and what lies before us are tiny matters compared to what lies within us." – *Ralph Waldo Emerson*

Insight

Self-as-context reminds you that you are more than your thoughts, feelings, and experiences. You are the constant observer of all these internal and external events.

Task

Take a moment today to observe your thoughts and feelings. See if you can step back and notice them without identifying with them. You are the one who notices, not the thoughts themselves.

Metaphor

The Sky and the Weather – You are like the sky, and your thoughts and emotions are like the weather. No matter what storms may pass, you remain vast and unchanging.

March 5

Quote

"The way to get started is to quit talking and begin doing." – *Walt Disney*

Insight

Procrastination often arises from overthinking. Committed action invites you to take that first step, even when things feel uncertain or overwhelming.

Task

Choose one task you've been putting off. Take a small action today to move it forward, no matter how imperfect the first step may be.

Metaphor

The Swing – Getting started is like pushing a swing. At first, it takes effort, but once the swing is in motion, it moves more easily. Action creates momentum.

March 6

Quote

"There is only one way to happiness, and that is to cease worrying about things which are beyond the power of our will." – *Epictetus*

Insight

Acceptance involves recognising what you cannot control and choosing not to waste your energy on it. This frees you to focus on what you can influence, bringing greater peace and effectiveness.

Task

Reflect on one area of your life where you've been trying to control the uncontrollable. Practice letting go of that need for control today and focus on what you can change instead.

Metaphor

The Tug of War – Life is like a game of tug-of-war with a monster on the other side. Acceptance is like dropping the rope. You stop the struggle and free yourself to focus on what truly matters.

March 7

Quote

"We are what we repeatedly do. Excellence, then, is not an act, but a habit." – *Aristotle*

Insight

Committed action is about consistency over time. It's not about grand gestures, but about taking small, value-driven actions repeatedly, which compound into meaningful change.

Task

Choose one habit that aligns with your values. Make a commitment to take one small action each day to nurture that habit, starting today.

Metaphor

The Brick Wall – Building a habit is like building a brick wall. Each small action is like laying a brick. Over time, those bricks build a strong, stable structure.

March 8

Quote

"Do not let what you cannot do interfere with what you can do." – *John Wooden*

Insight

When faced with limitations, it's easy to feel stuck. Defusion helps you separate from limiting thoughts, allowing you to focus on what you *can* do instead.

Task

Notice any thoughts today that tell you "I can't" or "I'm not able." Practice defusing from those thoughts by saying, "I'm having the thought that I can't," and then take action anyway.

Metaphor

The Thought Cloud – Limiting thoughts are like clouds passing through the sky. They may obscure your view for a moment, but they're temporary and will pass. You can still act in the direction of your values.

March 9

Quote

"Success is not how high you have climbed, but how you make a positive difference to the world." – *Roy T. Bennett*

Insight

A rich and meaningful life is not defined by external achievements, but by living in alignment with your values and contributing to something greater than yourself.

Task

Reflect on what "success" means to you. How does this definition align with your core values? Take one action today that reflects your true vision of success, beyond external measures.

Metaphor

The Ripple Effect – Success is like dropping a stone into a pond. The ripples you create by living in line with your values spread out, touching the lives of others in ways you may never see.

March 10: ADHD

Quote

"If a cluttered desk is a sign of a cluttered mind, of what, then, is an empty desk a sign?" – *Albert Einstein*

Insight

ADHD often involves difficulty with focus and organisation. Acceptance and self-compassion allow you to embrace your unique brain while finding ways to manage distractions.

Task

Today, focus on one task at a time. Use a timer for short bursts of focused work (e.g., 15 or 20 minutes), followed by a short break. See how this method impacts your ability to concentrate.

Metaphor

The Spotlight – Your attention is like a spotlight on a stage. ADHD can cause that spotlight to jump around, but with mindfulness and focus, you can guide it back to where you need it.

March 11

Quote

"Knowing others is intelligence; knowing yourself is true wisdom." – *Lao Tzu*

Insight

Self-awareness is key to a rich and meaningful life. Self-as-context helps you recognise that you are more than your thoughts, and by cultivating this awareness, you navigate life with greater clarity.

Task

Take five minutes today to practice mindfulness. Focus on your breath or your surroundings, and simply observe without judgement. Notice how this shifts your perspective on yourself and your experiences.

Metaphor

The Observer – You are like the observer in a theatre, watching the play of your thoughts and emotions unfold. By observing without attachment, you create space for calm and clarity.

March 12

Quote

"You can't stop the waves, but you can learn to surf." – *Jon Kabat-Zinn*

Insight

Acceptance means learning to ride the ups and downs of life, rather than trying to eliminate them. By embracing the reality of change, you find greater ease and resilience.

Task

Identify one difficult emotion you've been experiencing. Practice accepting that emotion today, without trying to push it away or fix it. See how your experience shifts when you allow the emotion to be.

Metaphor

The Ocean – Life is like the ocean, full of waves that rise and fall. By learning to surf these emotional waves rather than fight them, you find balance and flow.

March 13

Quote

"To know oneself is to study oneself in action with another person." – *Bruce Lee*

Insight

Self-awareness deepens through your interactions with others. Committed action means bringing your values into your relationships, even when it's challenging or uncomfortable.

Task

Reflect on one relationship that is important to you. What value do you want to embody in this relationship? Take one action today that expresses that value, no matter how small.

Metaphor

The Mirror – Relationships are like mirrors, reflecting back to us who we are. By acting in line with your values in your relationships, you not only grow yourself, but you also strengthen your connections.

March 14

Quote

"We must accept finite disappointment, but never lose infinite hope." – *Martin Luther King Jr.*

Insight

Acceptance doesn't mean giving up; it means acknowledging reality while continuing to move forward with hope and action aligned to your values.

Task

Identify a recent disappointment. Practice accepting it fully without losing sight of your hopes. What small action can you take today to move in the direction of your hopes?

Metaphor

The Compass – Acceptance is like recognising your true position on a map, while your values act like a compass, guiding you toward what matters most, no matter the setbacks.

March 15

Quote

"It is never too late to be what you might have been." – *George Eliot*

Insight

Defusion helps you separate from the limiting thoughts that hold you back. You are not defined by your past or your failures, but by the actions you choose today.

Task

Notice any limiting thoughts that arise today (e.g., "It's too late" or "I can't"). Defuse from them by saying, "I'm having the thought that..." and then take a value-driven action anyway.

Metaphor

Passengers on the Bus – Imagine your mind is like a bus, with unhelpful thoughts as passengers. You can let them chatter in the background without letting them control where you drive the bus.

March 16

Quote

"You miss 100% of the shots you don't take." – *Wayne Gretzky*

Insight

Committed action is about being willing to take risks and make mistakes in the pursuit of your values. Action, even imperfect, moves you closer to where you want to be.

Task

Think of one area in your life where you've been hesitant to take action due to fear of failure. Take one small step today, no matter how imperfect.

Metaphor

The Dartboard – Think of your values as a dartboard. Each time you take action, you throw a dart. Even if you don't hit the bullseye, each throw brings you closer to your target.

March 17: Anger

Quote

"Holding onto anger is like drinking poison and expecting the other person to die." – *Buddha*

Insight

Anger is a normal human emotion, but when held onto, it becomes harmful to you. Acceptance doesn't mean condoning what caused your anger, but it helps you let go of its grip on you.

Task

Identify one situation today that triggers anger. Practice noticing the anger without acting on it, and see if you can accept it without fuelling it further.

Metaphor

The Hot Coal – Holding onto anger is like holding a hot coal. The more you cling to it, the more you burn yourself. Letting go frees you from that pain.

March 18

Quote

"Life is 10% what happens to you and 90% how you react to it." – *Charles R. Swindoll*

Insight

Present-moment awareness helps you recognise that while you can't always control events, you can choose how you respond. With mindfulness, you can respond intentionally rather than react impulsively.

Task

Pay attention to how you respond to a challenging situation today. Before reacting, take a breath and pause. Notice how this changes your response.

Metaphor

The Pause Button – Mindfulness is like having a pause button for your reactions. It allows you to step back, reflect, and choose how you want to respond, rather than acting on autopilot.

March 19

Quote

"It is not the mountain we conquer but ourselves." – *Edmund Hillary*

Insight

Self-as-context helps you see that the greatest journey is the one within. By knowing yourself as the observer of your experiences, you build inner strength and resilience.

Task

Spend five minutes today in self-reflection. Observe your thoughts, emotions, and sensations without judgement. Notice the part of you that observes, and recognise its unshakable stability.

Metaphor

The Mountain – The challenges of life are like mountains, but the real journey is within. By knowing yourself as the unshakable observer, you can climb any mountain.

March 20

Quote

"There is no greater agony than bearing an untold story inside you." – *Maya Angelou*

Insight

Living a rich and meaningful life often involves expressing your authentic self. Committed action invites you to live in a way that reflects your inner truth, even when it's scary.

Task

What is one part of yourself that you've been holding back? Take a small step today to express that part of yourself, whether through writing, speaking, or action.

Metaphor

The Candle – Your authentic self is like a candle. When you hide it, you live in darkness. But when you let it shine, it brings light to you and those around you.

March 21

Quote

"We become what we think about." – *Earl Nightingale*

Insight

Defusion helps you separate from unhelpful thoughts, recognising that they do not define you. You are not your thoughts; you are the observer of your thoughts.

Task

Notice one repetitive, negative thought you've been having. Practice defusing from it by saying, "I'm having the thought that…" and observe how this changes your relationship to the thought.

Metaphor

Leaves on a Stream – Imagine your thoughts as leaves floating down a stream. You don't need to grab onto them or push them away; just let them float by as you observe from the shore.

March 22: Stress

Quote

"Stress is caused by being 'here' but wanting to be 'there.'" – *Eckhart Tolle*

Insight

Stress often comes from resisting the present moment, wishing things were different. Present-moment awareness invites you to be fully here, reducing the tension caused by that resistance.

Task

Practice mindfulness today by focusing on your breath for one minute. Each time your mind wanders, gently bring it back to the breath. Notice how this practice impacts your stress levels.

Metaphor

The Present Moment Anchor – The present moment is like an anchor that keeps you grounded. When you're caught in the storm of stress, returning to the present moment helps you stay steady and calm.

March 23

Quote

"The only way to make sense out of change is to plunge into it, move with it, and join the dance." – *Alan Watts*

Insight

Acceptance is about embracing change rather than resisting it. Life is constantly evolving, and by flowing with change, you find peace and resilience.

Task

Identify one change you've been resisting. Practice accepting it today by focusing on how you can adapt and grow from it, rather than trying to control or avoid it.

Metaphor

The Dance – Life is like a dance, always moving. By accepting the rhythm of change and learning to dance with it, you find grace and ease, even in uncertain times.

March 24

Quote

"Success is not final, failure is not fatal: It is the courage to continue that counts." – *Winston Churchill*

Insight

Committed action is about persistence in the face of setbacks. Each time you take action, no matter the outcome, you grow and move closer to living in alignment with your values.

Task

Think of one goal where you've faced setbacks. What's one small, courageous action you can take today to keep moving forward?

Metaphor

The Road – Success and failure are both part of the road to a meaningful life. Each step you take, whether a stumble or a stride, moves you further down that road.

March 25

Quote

"Not everything that is faced can be changed, but nothing can be changed until it is faced." – *James Baldwin*

Insight

Acceptance means facing reality as it is, without denying or avoiding it. Once you accept what is, you open the door to meaningful action and change.

Task

What's one reality you've been avoiding? Practice accepting it fully today, and then consider what small action you can take in response.

Metaphor

The Weather – Life's challenges are like the weather. You can't change the rain by ignoring it, but once you accept it's raining, you can choose to grab an umbrella and take action.

March 26

Quote

"You don't have to control your thoughts; you just have to stop letting them control you." – *Dan Millman*

Insight

Defusion teaches you that you can have thoughts without being ruled by them. You can observe them, let them be, and still act in line with your values.

Task

When a difficult thought arises today, practice observing it from a distance, without reacting. Imagine placing it on a cloud and letting it drift by, as you refocus on what matters to you.

Metaphor

The Thought Train – Your thoughts are like trains passing through a station. You can choose to observe them without boarding every train, allowing them to pass without pulling you off track.

March 27

Quote

"Everything you want is on the other side of fear." – *Jack Canfield*

Insight

Committed action is about moving toward your values, even when fear shows up. Fear is part of the journey, but it doesn't have to stop you from living a rich and meaningful life.

Task

Identify one fear that's been holding you back. Take one small step today in the direction of your values, despite the fear. Notice how courage builds through action.

Metaphor

The Fear Barrier – Imagine fear as a fog. By walking through the fog, step by step, you move closer to the life you want, even though you can't always see clearly.

March 28: ADHD

Quote

"Small daily improvements are the key to staggering long-term results." – *Robin Sharma*

Insight

Living with ADHD can make long-term goals feel overwhelming. Focus on small, manageable actions each day that align with your values, building momentum and progress over time.

Task

Pick one small, value-driven action today that you can complete. Break it into steps, and celebrate each small win as progress toward your larger goals.

Metaphor

The Brick Wall – Building a meaningful life is like constructing a wall. Each small, daily action is a brick, and over time, these bricks create something strong and enduring.

March 29

Quote

"The only journey is the one within." – *Rainer Maria Rilke*

Insight

Self-as-context teaches you to observe your inner experiences without getting lost in them. By cultivating this observer self, you gain perspective on life's challenges and your responses to them.

Task

Take a few minutes today to observe your thoughts and feelings without judgement. Notice the part of you that is always observing, steady and unchanging, amidst the flow of experiences.

Metaphor

The Sky – Your mind is like the sky, vast and unchanging. Your thoughts and feelings are like weather patterns, constantly shifting. The sky remains unchanged no matter the storm.

March 30: Addiction

Quote

"Recovery is not for people who need it; it's for people who want it." – *Anonymous*

Insight

Committed action in the face of addiction requires a deep connection to your values. Recovery is not about perfection but persistence in the direction of what truly matters to you.

Task

Reflect on what you value most in life. What is one small action you can take today that supports your recovery and aligns with those values?

Metaphor

The Lighthouse – Recovery is like a lighthouse, guiding you through the storm. Your values are the light, helping you navigate difficult moments and stay on course toward a meaningful life.

March 31

Quote

"The secret of change is to focus all of your energy not on fighting the old, but on building the new." – *Socrates*

Insight

Acceptance is about letting go of the struggle with what's past and focusing instead on creating the future you want. By committing to your values, you build the life that matters to you.

Task

What's one old struggle or pattern you've been holding onto? Practice letting it go today, and shift your energy toward a value-driven action that builds the future you want.

Metaphor

The Garden – Letting go of old patterns is like pulling weeds from a garden. As you clear away what no longer serves you, you make space for new growth and possibilities

APRIL

April 1

Quote

"Success is to be measured not so much by the position that one has reached in life as by the obstacles which he has overcome." – *Booker T. Washington*

Insight

Committed action isn't just about achieving results, but about the persistence and courage you show in overcoming challenges on your journey toward your values.

Task

Reflect on one challenge you have recently faced. What strengths or skills did you use to move through it? Acknowledge yourself for your persistence.

Metaphor

The Mountain Climb – The path to success is like climbing a mountain. Progress isn't just about reaching the summit, but about how you handle the difficult terrain along the way.

April 2

Quote

"Life is what happens when you're busy making other plans."
– John Lennon

Insight

Present-moment awareness teaches you that while it's important to plan, life is lived in the present. By being fully engaged in the here and now, you enrich your daily experience.

Task

Today, bring your full attention to one routine activity (e.g., brushing your teeth, having a meal). Notice the sensations, thoughts, and emotions that arise as you engage fully in the present.

Metaphor

The Now – Life is like a book, and each moment is a new page. If you're too focused on the end, you'll miss the richness of the story unfolding in front of you.

April 3

Quote

"To be yourself in a world that is constantly trying to make you something else is the greatest accomplishment." – *Ralph Waldo Emerson*

Insight

Living authentically requires defusion from societal pressures and expectations. By staying connected to your values, you find the strength to be your true self, despite external influences.

Task

Identify one value that is important to you, and take one small action today that reflects that value, regardless of how others may respond.

Metaphor

The Tree – Your values are like the roots of a tree. While the winds of social pressure may blow, a tree firmly grounded in its roots remains steady and strong.

April 4

Quote

"The best way out is always through." – *Robert Frost*

Insight

Acceptance invites you to move through discomfort rather than avoiding it. By facing and accepting difficult experiences, you develop resilience and discover new strengths.

Task

Identify one uncomfortable emotion you've been avoiding. Today, practice accepting it fully without judgement. Allow it to be present and notice how it changes over time.

Metaphor

The Tunnel – Acceptance is like walking through a tunnel. The only way to the other side is to go through it, trusting that light will come as you move forward.

April 5

Quote

"I am not what happened to me, I am what I choose to become." – *Carl Jung*

Insight

Self-as-context helps you see that your identity is not defined by past events or labels. You are the observer of your experiences, and you have the power to choose how you respond to them.

Task

Spend a few moments reflecting on a difficult experience. Notice the part of you that observes this experience, steady and unchanged. Recognise that while the event happened, it does not define who you are.

Metaphor

The Riverbank – Your life experiences are like a river flowing past, and you are standing on the bank, watching them go by. No matter how strong the current, you remain the stable observer.

April 6

Quote

"Courage doesn't always roar. Sometimes courage is the quiet voice at the end of the day saying, 'I will try again tomorrow.'" – *Mary Anne Radmacher*

Insight

Committed action doesn't require grand gestures. Sometimes it's about showing up again, even when the day has been tough. Each small step in line with your values is a success.

Task

Think of one area where you've struggled to make progress. What is one small action you can take today to move closer to your goal? Commit to that action, no matter how small.

Metaphor

The Pebble – Progress is like dropping pebbles into a jar. Each small action adds up over time, and soon the jar is full, even if each pebble feels insignificant on its own.

April 7

Quote

"Your life does not get better by chance, it gets better by change." – *Jim Rohn*

Insight

Defusion helps you see that waiting for external circumstances to change isn't enough. By changing your relationship to your thoughts and taking committed action, you create the life you want.

Task

What is one unhelpful thought that's been holding you back? Practice defusing from it today by saying, "I'm having the thought that…" and take a small step toward your goal despite the thought.

Metaphor

The Inner Landscape – Your thoughts are like weather passing through your inner landscape. Just as you don't control the weather, you don't control your thoughts, but you can choose how to navigate the storm.

April 8: Anger

Quote

"For every minute you remain angry, you give up sixty seconds of peace of mind." – *Ralph Waldo Emerson*

Insight

Anger often arises when things don't go our way, but holding onto anger prolongs our suffering. Acceptance helps you release the struggle and find peace, even when things are difficult.

Task

Notice when anger arises today. Take a moment to breathe and ask yourself if holding onto the anger serves you. Practice releasing it and notice how your peace increases.

Metaphor

The Hot Coal – Anger is like holding onto a hot coal, expecting it to burn someone else. The longer you hold it, the more you get burned. Letting go frees you from the heat.

April 9

Quote

"He who has a why to live can bear almost any how." – *Friedrich Nietzsche*

Insight

Values provide a powerful "why" that gives you the strength to endure difficulties. By staying connected to your values, you find meaning in even the most challenging circumstances.

Task

Identify one of your core values and reflect on how it has helped you through tough times. Consider how you can reconnect with this value today in a meaningful way.

Metaphor

The North Star – Your values are like the North Star, guiding you through life's challenges. No matter how dark the night or stormy the sea, the North Star remains a constant point of reference.

April 10

Quote

"No act of kindness, no matter how small, is ever wasted." – *Aesop*

Insight

Committed action doesn't always have to be big or grand. Small, value-driven acts of kindness can make a profound difference in both your life and the lives of others.

Task

Perform one small act of kindness today, whether for a stranger, a loved one, or yourself. Notice how this simple action aligns with your values and enriches your day.

Metaphor

The Ripple – Kindness is like a stone dropped into a pond. The ripples spread outward, touching the lives of others in ways you may not even see, but the impact endures.

April 11: Stress

Quote

"Sometimes the most productive thing you can do is relax." – *Mark Black*

Insight

In moments of stress, it's easy to feel that doing more will solve the problem. However, learning to pause and relax can be the most effective way to manage stress and restore balance.

Task

Take 5-10 minutes today to practise relaxation. This could be through deep breathing, meditation, or simply sitting quietly. Notice how giving yourself permission to relax helps reduce stress.

Metaphor

The Bowstring – Life is like a bow. If you constantly keep it drawn, the tension will eventually break it. By periodically releasing the tension, you maintain your strength and resilience.

April 12

Quote

"The only limit to our realisation of tomorrow is our doubts of today." – *Franklin D. Roosevelt*

Insight

Defusion helps you recognise that doubts are just thoughts, not truths. By separating yourself from your doubts, you can move forward with confidence and take action toward your goals.

Task

Notice one doubt that's been holding you back. Practise defusion by saying, "I'm having the thought that…" and then take one small action in the direction of your goals, despite the doubt.

Metaphor

The Fog of Doubt – Doubts are like fog on the road. They may obscure your vision, but they don't stop the road from being there. By moving forward, you will eventually emerge from the fog.

April 13

Quote

"It is never too late to be what you might have been." – *George Eliot*

Insight

Self-as-context reminds you that you are not defined by your past choices. You are always capable of choosing a new path and taking committed action toward your values, no matter where you start.

Task

Reflect on one area of your life where you've felt it's "too late" to make a change. What's one small step you can take today to begin moving in the direction of your values?

Metaphor

The Compass – Your past is like the terrain you've already travelled, but your values are the compass guiding you forward. No matter where you are, you can always reorient toward a meaningful path.

April 14

Quote

"Do not dwell in the past, do not dream of the future, concentrate the mind on the present moment." – *Buddha*

Insight

Present-moment awareness allows you to fully experience life as it unfolds. By letting go of ruminations about the past and worries about the future, you create space for joy and growth in the present.

Task

Spend five minutes today practising mindful breathing. Each time your mind wanders, gently bring your attention back to the sensation of your breath, anchoring yourself in the present moment.

Metaphor

The Anchor – Your breath is like an anchor, holding you steady in the present moment amidst the waves of thoughts and emotions.

April 15

Quote

"To forgive is to set a prisoner free and discover that the prisoner was you." – *Lewis B. Smedes*

Insight

Acceptance is not about condoning what happened, but about freeing yourself from the burden of holding onto pain. When you accept and release past hurts, you open the door to healing and peace.

Task

Reflect on one past event or person you've been holding resentment toward. Practise self-compassion as you begin to let go of that resentment. Notice the lightness that comes from releasing it.

Metaphor

The Heavy Backpack – Carrying resentment is like carrying a heavy backpack. The longer you carry it, the more exhausted you become. By letting it go, you free yourself to move more lightly through life.

April 16

Quote

"We are what we repeatedly do. Excellence, then, is not an act, but a habit." – *Aristotle*

Insight

Committed action is about consistency in your value-driven actions. Each small step, repeated regularly, builds the habits that lead to long-term success and fulfilment.

Task

Identify one small habit that aligns with your values. Commit to practising it each day for the next week, no matter how small. Celebrate your progress as you build consistency.

Metaphor

The Seedling – Building habits is like planting a seed. With regular care and attention, it grows steadily into something strong and enduring.

April 17: Apathy

Quote

"The price of apathy towards public affairs is to be ruled by evil men." – *Plato*

Insight

Apathy arises when you disconnect from your values. Reconnecting with what matters most to you can reignite a sense of purpose and inspire meaningful action, even in the face of indifference.

Task

Spend time today reflecting on your values. What do you care deeply about, even if it feels distant right now? Take one small action today that aligns with those values.

Metaphor

The Flame – Apathy is like a flame that has dimmed. By reconnecting with your values and nurturing them, you reignite the fire of purpose and passion.

April 18

Quote

"Our greatest glory is not in never falling, but in rising every time we fall." – *Confucius*

Insight

Self-as-context teaches you that your worth is not defined by your successes or failures. You are the observer of your experiences, capable of learning and growing from each one.

Task

Reflect on a recent failure or setback. Notice how you are the observer of this event, not defined by it. What have you learned from this experience, and how can you use it to move forward?

Metaphor

The Phoenix – Your experiences are like the ashes from which you can rise, stronger and wiser. Each setback is an opportunity for growth and transformation.

April 19

Quote

"You miss 100% of the shots you don't take." – *Wayne Gretzky*

Insight

Defusion helps you notice when fear of failure or self-doubt is holding you back. By observing these thoughts without letting them control you, you free yourself to take action and pursue your goals.

Task

Identify one opportunity you've been avoiding because of fear or doubt. Practise defusion by saying, "I'm having the thought that I might fail…" Then take one small step toward that opportunity today.

Metaphor

The Open Door – Opportunities are like open doors. Doubts may whisper that the door will close before you reach it, but by moving forward, you increase your chances of walking through.

April 20

Quote

"The wound is the place where the Light enters you." – *Rumi*

Insight

Acceptance doesn't mean you enjoy or welcome pain, but it allows you to see that even in the most difficult experiences, there is the potential for growth, learning, and healing.

Task

Think of a painful experience you've been resisting. Practise acceptance by allowing yourself to feel the discomfort without trying to change or control it. Notice what insights or strengths emerge from this process.

Metaphor

The Broken Pot – Painful experiences are like cracks in a pot. Through those cracks, light and wisdom can shine, illuminating new paths forward.

April 21

Quote

"Life isn't about finding yourself. Life is about creating yourself." – *George Bernard Shaw*

Insight

Committed action reminds you that life is not a passive experience but one you actively create through your choices. By aligning your actions with your values, you become the author of your own life story.

Task

What is one area of your life where you feel passive or stuck? Take one value-driven action today, no matter how small, to begin creating the life you want in that area.

Metaphor

The Sculptor – You are the sculptor of your life. Each value-driven action is like a chisel stroke, shaping and refining the person you are becoming.

April 22: Stress

Quote

"Tension is who you think you should be. Relaxation is who you are." – *Chinese Proverb*

Insight

Stress often arises when you are caught in striving to meet external expectations. Present-moment awareness allows you to return to your true self, reconnecting with peace and authenticity.

Task

Spend a few minutes today sitting quietly, focusing on your breath. As you breathe, let go of any tension or pressure you're holding onto. Allow yourself to just be in this moment, as you are.

Metaphor

The Balloon – Stress is like inflating a balloon. If you keep blowing air into it, eventually it will burst. By letting go of some of the air (expectations), you relieve the pressure and prevent burnout.

April 23

Quote

"What lies behind us and what lies before us are tiny matters compared to what lies within us." – *Ralph Waldo Emerson*

Insight

Self-as-context reminds you that while external circumstances change, your inner strength and values remain a constant source of guidance. By connecting with your inner self, you tap into a well of resilience.

Task

Reflect on a recent challenge. Spend time connecting with the part of you that observes this challenge from a steady, grounded place. How does this perspective help you approach the situation differently?

Metaphor

The Rock – Your true self is like a rock in the middle of a river. The water (challenges) flows around it, but the rock remains unmoved, strong, and enduring.

April 24

Quote

"Act as if what you do makes a difference. It does." – *William James*

Insight

Committed action is about recognising that each action you take, no matter how small, contributes to the life you are building. By consistently acting in line with your values, you create meaningful change.

Task

Choose one value-driven action today that seems small or insignificant. Complete it with full awareness, knowing that even small actions build the foundation for a rich and meaningful life.

Metaphor

The Drops in a Bucket – Each action is like a drop of water added to a bucket. Over time, these small drops accumulate, filling the bucket and creating something substantial.

April 25

Quote

"In three words I can sum up everything I've learned about life: It goes on." – *Robert Frost*

Insight

Present-moment awareness allows you to see that life is constantly flowing. By accepting this truth, you become more adaptable to change and able to navigate life's challenges with grace.

Task

Spend a few moments today observing the transient nature of your thoughts and feelings. Notice how they arise, stay for a while, and pass. Reflect on how this impermanence allows life to move forward.

Metaphor

The River – Life is like a river that flows continuously. By accepting the current rather than resisting it, you move more easily with the natural flow of life.

April 26: Addiction

Quote

"First we make our habits, then our habits make us." – *Charles C. Noble*

Insight

Defusion helps you notice urges without being controlled by them. Recognising that urges are just thoughts or sensations gives you the freedom to choose actions aligned with your values rather than giving in to habits that don't serve you.

Task

Notice one urge today that doesn't align with your values. Practise defusion by labelling it as, "I'm having the urge to…" and then choose an action that moves you toward your values.

Metaphor

The Bus Driver – Your mind is like a bus filled with passengers (urges, thoughts). You're the driver, and while you can hear the passengers, it's up to you where to steer the bus.

April 27

Quote

"Courage is resistance to fear, mastery of fear, not absence of fear." – *Mark Twain*

Insight

Acceptance involves making space for uncomfortable emotions, such as fear, rather than trying to push them away. By embracing fear, you can still take meaningful action in the direction of your values.

Task

Reflect on a fear you've been avoiding. What value lies behind this fear? Take one small action today that moves you closer to that value, even if the fear is still present.

Metaphor

The Passenger – Fear is like a passenger in your car. It doesn't need to sit in the driver's seat, but it can ride along as you continue toward your destination.

April 28

Quote

"What we achieve inwardly will change outer reality." – *Plutarch*

Insight

Self-as-context reminds you that the way you see yourself can influence your external life. By connecting with your inner observer, you gain the clarity and strength to create change in the outer world.

Task

Spend time today connecting with your inner observer. Who are you at your core, beyond your thoughts and emotions? How does this perspective help you approach life's challenges with more clarity?

Metaphor

The Mirror – Your self-concept is like a mirror. When the surface is clouded by thoughts and emotions, it's harder to see clearly. By cleaning the mirror (self-reflection), you gain a clearer view of who you truly are.

April 29: ADHD

Quote

"Focus is not about saying yes. It's about saying no." – *Steve Jobs*

Insight

Present-moment awareness can be challenging for those with ADHD, but learning to gently bring your attention back to the task at hand can help. Focus isn't about maintaining perfect attention but about continually refocusing when distractions arise.

Task

Choose a task today that requires focus. Set a timer for 10-15 minutes and commit to working on it without distractions. If your mind wanders, gently bring it back to the present moment and continue.

Metaphor

The Spotlight – Your attention is like a spotlight on a stage. It can move around, but with practice, you can direct it to shine where you want it to go.

April 30

Quote

"Success is not final, failure is not fatal: It is the courage to continue that counts." – *Winston Churchill*

Insight

Committed action is about resilience and persistence. Whether you experience success or failure, what matters most is your ability to keep moving forward in the direction of your values.

Task

Think of a recent success or failure. How can you continue building on the success or learning from the failure? Take one action today that moves you further along your path.

Metaphor

The Tapestry – Life is like a tapestry woven from both successes and failures. Each thread adds to the beauty and complexity of the whole, no matter its colour or texture.

MAY

May 1

Quote

"The journey of a thousand miles begins with one step." – *Lao Tzu*

Insight

Committed action doesn't have to be grand. Often, the most important part is just starting. By taking small, consistent steps toward your values, you make progress on your journey.

Task

Think of a long-term goal or value that feels overwhelming. Identify the smallest possible step you can take today in that direction. Take that step, knowing that it's moving you forward.

Metaphor

The Staircase – Moving toward your goals is like climbing a staircase. Each small step brings you higher, even if the top seems far away. Every step counts.

May 2

Quote

"Life is 10% what happens to us and 90% how we react to it."
– *Charles R. Swindoll*

Insight

Acceptance doesn't mean you like or agree with everything that happens, but it allows you to choose how to respond. By accepting what you can't control, you gain the freedom to take meaningful action where it counts.

Task

Identify one situation today that is outside your control. Practise accepting it as it is, without resisting or wishing it were different. Then focus your energy on responding in a way that aligns with your values.

Metaphor

The Sailboat – Life is like sailing a boat. While you can't control the wind or the waves, you can adjust your sails and choose how to navigate through the storm.

May 3

Quote

"The best way out is always through." – *Robert Frost*

Insight

Present-moment awareness helps you stay grounded during difficult experiences. By staying with the discomfort rather than avoiding it, you build resilience and strength to move through life's challenges.

Task

Spend a few minutes today sitting with an uncomfortable thought or emotion without trying to change it. Breathe deeply and observe it from a place of acceptance. Notice how, over time, the discomfort shifts or diminishes.

Metaphor

The Storm – Difficult emotions are like a storm passing through the sky. The storm is temporary, but the sky remains. By staying present, you witness the storm without being consumed by it.

May 4

Quote

"You cannot swim for new horizons until you have courage to lose sight of the shore." – *William Faulkner*

Insight

Defusion helps you recognise when your mind is clinging to familiar, safe thoughts that keep you from growth. By noticing these thoughts and choosing not to be controlled by them, you open yourself to new possibilities.

Task

Identify one thought or belief today that has been holding you back. Practise defusion by saying, "I'm having the thought that…" and notice how this allows you to explore new actions without fear.

Metaphor

The Lifeboat – Your mind can be like a lifeboat that keeps you tied to familiar shores. Sometimes, real growth requires courage to leave the safety of the boat and swim toward new, meaningful horizons.

May 5: Anger

Quote

"For every minute you remain angry, you give up sixty seconds of peace of mind." – *Ralph Waldo Emerson*

Insight

Anger can be a powerful emotion, but holding onto it can prevent you from living according to your values. Acceptance allows you to experience anger without being consumed by it, making room for more constructive responses.

Task

Reflect on a recent moment of anger. Practise accepting the emotion without judgement. Notice how the intensity of the anger shifts when you make space for it rather than fighting it.

Metaphor

The Hot Coal – Holding onto anger is like holding a hot coal in your hand. The longer you hold it, the more you burn yourself. By setting it down, you free yourself from the pain.

May 6

Quote

"Happiness is not something ready made. It comes from your own actions." – *Dalai Lama*

Insight

Committed action is about choosing behaviours that align with your values, even when it's difficult. By consistently taking value-driven action, you create the conditions for happiness and fulfilment.

Task

Identify one value-driven action you've been avoiding because it feels difficult or uncomfortable. Take a small step today, knowing that happiness often follows from meaningful action, not the other way around.

Metaphor

The Garden – Happiness is like a garden. You can't expect flowers to grow without planting seeds and tending the soil. By taking action aligned with your values, you nurture the conditions for happiness to bloom.

May 7

Quote

"You have power over your mind—not outside events. Realise this, and you will find strength." – *Marcus Aurelius*

Insight

Self-as-context reminds you that you are not your thoughts, emotions, or external circumstances. You are the observer of these experiences, and by recognising this, you gain strength and freedom to act in alignment with your values.

Task

Spend a few moments today observing your thoughts and emotions without attaching to them. Notice how you are the observer, the steady centre, from which all these experiences arise and pass.

Metaphor

The Sky – Your thoughts and emotions are like clouds passing through the sky. No matter how turbulent or heavy they are, the sky (your true self) remains vast and unchanging

May 8

Quote

"We are what we repeatedly do. Excellence, then, is not an act, but a habit." – *Aristotle*

Insight

Committed action builds habits that align with your values. Small, consistent actions lead to lasting change and growth, creating a foundation for excellence in all areas of your life.

Task

Identify one small habit that aligns with your values. Commit to practising it every day for the next week, and notice how the habit begins to take root and influence your life.

Metaphor

The Snowball – Building habits is like rolling a snowball down a hill. At first, it's small and requires effort, but as it gains momentum, it grows larger and moves more easily on its own.

May 9: Stress

Quote

"Adopting the right attitude can convert a negative stress into a positive one." – *Hans Selye*

Insight

Present-moment awareness helps you manage stress by keeping you grounded in the here and now. Stress often arises from worrying about the future or ruminating on the past. By focusing on the present, you can respond more calmly and effectively.

Task

Spend five minutes today practising mindful breathing. Each time your mind wanders to a stressful thought, gently bring it back to your breath. Notice how this helps reduce stress and brings you back to the present moment.

Metaphor

The Wave – Stressful thoughts are like waves crashing on the shore. By staying grounded in the present moment, you become like the solid sand, allowing the waves to wash over without being swept away.

May 10

Quote

"You are never too old to set another goal or to dream a new dream." – C.S. Lewis

Insight

Self-as-context teaches you that no matter your age or circumstances, you always have the capacity to grow, change, and pursue new goals. You are not defined by your past, but by the choices you make in the present.

Task

Reflect on one goal or dream that you've set aside because it seemed "too late" to pursue. What's one small step you can take today to begin moving in the direction of that dream?

May 11

Quote

"Do not dwell in the past, do not dream of the future, concentrate the mind on the present moment." – *Buddha*

Insight

Present-moment awareness is a practice of returning your attention to the here and now. It allows you to fully engage with life as it unfolds, without getting lost in past regrets or future anxieties.

Task

Spend five minutes today practising mindful observation of your surroundings. Engage your senses fully—what do you see, hear, feel, or smell? Let this bring you into the present moment.

Metaphor

The Sand Timer – Time flows constantly, like sand through a timer. You can't hold onto the grains that have already passed, nor can you grasp those yet to come. All you have is the present.

May 12

Quote

"If you want to live a happy life, tie it to a goal, not to people or things." – *Albert Einstein*

Insight

Values provide a sense of purpose and direction that extends beyond external circumstances. By staying connected to your values, you build a meaningful life that isn't dependent on fleeting experiences or possessions.

Task

Reflect on one core value that has been important to you throughout your life. How can you incorporate that value more intentionally into your day-to-day actions?

Metaphor

The Compass – Your values are like a compass guiding you through life's challenges. While the path may change, your values help you stay true to your direction.

May 13: ADHD

Quote

"Small deeds done are better than great deeds planned." – *Peter Marshall*

Insight

For those with ADHD, tasks can feel overwhelming. Present-moment awareness and breaking tasks into small, manageable steps can help. Focus on taking action rather than getting caught up in planning or perfectionism.

Task

Pick one task that feels overwhelming today. Break it down into the smallest possible step, and focus only on completing that step. Celebrate your progress, no matter how small.

Metaphor

The Brick Wall – Building a wall can seem overwhelming, but if you focus on laying one brick at a time, eventually you'll create something solid and lasting.

May 14

Quote

"The only way to make sense out of change is to plunge into it, move with it, and join the dance." – *Alan Watts*

Insight

Acceptance allows you to flow with change rather than resist it. Life is full of uncertainty, but by embracing the unknown, you open yourself to new opportunities for growth and learning.

Task

Reflect on a recent change in your life. Practise accepting it as part of your journey, even if it's uncomfortable. How can you "join the dance" and move with this change rather than resist it?

Metaphor

The River – Life's changes are like a river's current. You can't stop the flow, but you can learn to swim with it, using the current to guide you forward.

May 15: Addiction

Quote

"Recovery is not for people who need it, it's for people who want it." – *Anonymous*

Insight

Committed action in recovery is about making value-driven choices. It's not about willpower alone but about being clear on your "why"—the values and purpose behind your desire for change.

Task

Identify one value that drives your recovery journey. Write down one small action you can take today that aligns with that value, and commit to it.

Metaphor

The Lighthouse – Your values in recovery are like a lighthouse guiding you through the storm. No matter how rough the seas get, the light remains steady, showing you the way forward.

May 16

Quote

"It is never too late to be what you might have been." – *George Eliot*

Insight

Self-as-context reminds you that you are not limited by your past. You are a dynamic, ever-evolving being, capable of growth and change at any stage in life. Your past does not define your future.

Task

Reflect on an old dream or ambition that you've set aside. What small step can you take today to move closer to that dream?

Metaphor

The Phoenix – Like a phoenix rising from the ashes, you have the power to reinvent yourself and pursue new paths, no matter where you are in life.

May 17

Quote

"You can't stop the waves, but you can learn to surf." – *Jon Kabat-Zinn*

Insight

Present-moment awareness helps you navigate life's challenges by accepting them without resistance. By staying present, you become more flexible and capable of adapting to whatever comes your way.

Task

Throughout the day, notice moments when you're resisting a difficult experience. Instead of pushing it away, practise staying present with it. Observe how this shifts your relationship with the challenge.

Metaphor

The Surfer – Life's challenges are like waves in the ocean. While you can't control them, you can learn to ride them, staying balanced and present no matter how rough the sea gets.

May 18

Quote

"Our greatest glory is not in never falling, but in rising every time we fall." – *Confucius*

Insight

Committed action is about persistence. It's not about never failing but about getting up and continuing on the path, no matter how many times you stumble. Your values guide you, even through setbacks.

Task

Reflect on a recent failure or setback. What can you learn from it? How can you rise again, taking a value-driven action that moves you forward?

Metaphor

The Rubber Ball – Like a rubber ball that bounces back after hitting the ground, you have the ability to rise again after every fall. The more you practise, the stronger your bounce becomes.

May 19

Quote

"What lies behind us and what lies before us are tiny matters compared to what lies within us." – *Ralph Waldo Emerson*

Insight

Self-as-context helps you recognise that your true strength and resilience come from within. By connecting with your inner self, you find the power to navigate both the past and the future with grace and confidence.

Task

Spend five minutes in quiet reflection today, connecting with your inner self. What qualities or strengths do you carry within you that help you face life's challenges?

Metaphor

The Anchor – Your inner self is like an anchor, grounding you through life's storms. No matter how rough the seas, the anchor keeps you steady and connected to what truly matters.

May 20

Quote

"Success is not the key to happiness. Happiness is the key to success. If you love what you are doing, you will be successful." – *Albert Schweitzer*

Insight

Values-driven action brings fulfilment, and true success comes from living in alignment with what you care about most. When you live according to your values, success becomes a natural byproduct of the joy and meaning you create.

Task

Reflect on one area of your life where you are seeking success. How can you shift your focus to the values underlying that pursuit? Take one action today that aligns with those values.

Metaphor

The Garden – Just as a gardener focuses on nurturing the soil and tending to the plants, success grows naturally when you focus on cultivating your values and joy in the process.

May 21: Fear

Quote

"The only thing we have to fear is fear itself." – *Franklin D. Roosevelt*

Insight

Defusion helps you distance yourself from fear-based thoughts. Instead of letting them control your actions, you can observe them from a distance, allowing you to move forward despite fear.

Task

Identify a fear-based thought that has been holding you back recently. Practise defusion by observing it as just a thought, without letting it control your next steps. What small action can you take despite this fear?

Metaphor

Passengers on a Bus – Imagine your fear-based thoughts as passengers on a bus. While they may be loud and demanding, you are the driver, and you decide the direction the bus takes.

May 22: Stress

Quote

"Tension is who you think you should be. Relaxation is who you are." – *Chinese Proverb*

Insight

Stress often arises from striving to meet external expectations or trying to control what's beyond your control. Acceptance allows you to release this tension, returning to a state of being where you can respond calmly and effectively.

Task

Identify one source of stress in your life. Practise acceptance by recognising what is within your control and what isn't. Let go of any need to control the uncontrollable, and focus your energy on what you can influence.

Metaphor

The Chinese Finger Trap – The harder you pull to escape a finger trap, the tighter it becomes. But by releasing tension, you find the freedom to break free. Similarly, acceptance helps you release the tension of stress.

May 23: Apathy

Quote

"The greatest glory in living lies not in never falling, but in rising every time we fall." – *Nelson Mandela*

Insight

Apathy can stem from feeling overwhelmed or disconnected from your values. By taking small, committed actions aligned with what truly matters to you, you can rekindle motivation and a sense of purpose.

Task

Identify one value that feels important to you but has been neglected. Take one small step today to engage with this value, even if it feels difficult.

Metaphor

The Seed – A seed can appear dormant but has the potential to grow into something beautiful. Similarly, taking even small actions can reignite your passion and motivation.

May 24: Growth

Quote

"What lies behind us and what lies before us are tiny matters compared to what lies within us." – *Ralph Waldo Emerson*

Insight

True growth comes from within. By nurturing your inner self and staying connected to your values, you can develop resilience and move forward despite external circumstances.

Task

Reflect on a challenge you've faced. What internal resources (strengths, values) helped you through? How can you draw on these resources for future challenges?

Metaphor

The Oak Tree – An oak tree grows strong by weathering storms. Similarly, your inner strength develops through overcoming challenges and nurturing your core values.

May 25: ADHD

Quote

"The secret of getting ahead is getting started." – *Mark Twain*

Insight

For those with ADHD, starting tasks can be a significant barrier. By focusing on just starting, even if it's a small step, you create momentum that can carry you forward.

Task

Pick a task you've been procrastinating on. Set a timer for five minutes and commit to just starting. Once the timer ends, decide if you want to continue or take a break. The key is to begin.

Metaphor

The Snowball – Starting can feel small, like a snowball, but as you keep rolling, it gains momentum and size. Just starting can create the momentum to keep going.

May 26: Commitment

Quote

"You are never too old to set another goal or to dream a new dream." – C.S. Lewis

Insight

Committed action is about setting meaningful goals that align with your values. It's never too late to pursue what matters to you and take steps towards your aspirations.

Task

Identify one goal that excites you. Break it down into smaller, actionable steps, and commit to taking the first step today.

Metaphor

The Compass – Your values are like a compass, guiding you towards your true north. Even small steps in the right direction can lead to significant changes over time.

May 27: Acceptance

Quote

"Acceptance does not mean resignation; it means understanding that something is what it is and that there's got to be a way through it." – *Michael J. Fox*

Insight

Acceptance allows you to face reality without resistance. It doesn't mean you approve of what's happening; rather, it helps you find clarity and direction amidst challenges.

Task

Identify a situation in your life that feels difficult. Practise acceptance by acknowledging it as it is, without trying to change it immediately. What clarity does this bring?

Metaphor

The River – Like a river flowing past obstacles, acceptance allows you to move around challenges instead of getting stuck. You can still navigate your course, even when facing difficulties.

May 28: Anger

Quote

"For every minute you are angry, you lose sixty seconds of happiness." – *Ralph Waldo Emerson*

Insight

Anger is a normal emotion, but holding onto it can rob you of joy. Acceptance helps you acknowledge your anger without letting it control your actions, allowing you to return to a place of peace.

Task

Next time you feel angry, pause and breathe. Rather than acting on your anger, practise acceptance by noticing the sensations in your body without judgement.

Metaphor

The Volcano – Anger is like a volcano. If you ignore it or suppress it, it will eventually erupt. By acknowledging and accepting your anger, you allow the pressure to release safely.

May 29: Apathy

Quote

"The greatest glory in living lies not in never falling, but in rising every time we fall." – *Nelson Mandela*

Insight

Apathy can stem from feeling overwhelmed or disconnected from your values. By taking small, committed actions aligned with what truly matters to you, you can rekindle motivation and a sense of purpose.

Task

Identify one value that feels important to you but has been neglected. Take one small step today to engage with this value, even if it feels difficult.

Metaphor

The Seed – A seed can appear dormant but has the potential to grow into something beautiful. Similarly, taking even small actions can reignite your passion and motivation.

May 30: Success

Quote

"Success is not the key to happiness. Happiness is the key to success. If you love what you are doing, you will be successful." – *Albert Schweitzer*

Insight

Success is deeply intertwined with your values. When you pursue what truly matters to you, your actions become meaningful, leading to authentic success.

Task

Reflect on what success means to you. Write down three values that guide your definition of success, and identify one action you can take today that aligns with these values.

Metaphor

The Lighthouse – Like a lighthouse guiding ships to shore, your values guide you toward your version of success. Stay anchored to these values as you navigate life's waters.

May 31: Growth

Quote

"You cannot change your future, but you can change your habits, and surely your habits will change your future." – *Jim Rohn*

Insight

Growth is a continuous process that involves developing new habits aligned with your values. Each small change you make today can lead to significant transformations over time.

Task

Identify one habit you would like to cultivate that aligns with your values. Outline a plan for integrating this habit into your daily routine, starting with one small action you can take today.

Metaphor

The Garden – Just as a garden flourishes with consistent care, your growth requires nurturing and attention. By tending to your habits, you can cultivate a rich and fulfilling life.

JUNE

June 1: Values

Quote

"Your values create your actions, your actions create your habits, and your habits create your future." – *Unknown*

Insight

Understanding your core values provides a foundation for meaningful action. When you live in alignment with your values, your life becomes more purposeful and fulfilling.

Task

List your top three values. Reflect on how your recent actions align with these values. What is one action you can take this week to further align your life with your values?

Metaphor

The Compass – Your values act as a compass, guiding you through the complexities of life. When you stay true to them, you navigate with confidence and direction.

June 2: Acceptance

Quote

"The greatest gift you can give yourself is the gift of unconditional love." – *Brian Tracy*

Insight

Acceptance involves recognising your feelings and experiences without judgement. By offering yourself compassion and understanding, you create space for healing and growth.

Task

Choose one emotion you find difficult to accept. Write down how this emotion feels in your body. Practise accepting it without judgement for a few minutes today.

Metaphor

The Balloon – Imagine holding a balloon filled with air (your emotions). By accepting and acknowledging the air, the balloon stays buoyant. If you resist it, the pressure builds up until it pops.

June 3: Present Moment Awareness

Quote

"Realise deeply that the present moment is all you ever have."
– *Eckhart Tolle*

Insight

Being present allows you to experience life fully. When you focus on the here and now, you can appreciate each moment without being bogged down by past regrets or future anxieties.

Task

Set aside five minutes today for mindfulness. Focus on your breath or your surroundings, allowing yourself to experience the present moment without distraction.

Metaphor

The Still Water – Like a pond that reflects the sky perfectly when still, your mind reflects your experiences best when calm and present. Embrace the clarity of the moment.

June 4: Defusion

Quote

"You are not your thoughts." – *Unknown*

Insight

Defusion techniques help you separate yourself from your thoughts, allowing you to observe them without judgement. This practice empowers you to respond to life rather than react impulsively.

Task

Choose a thought that troubles you. Visualise it as a leaf floating down a stream. Watch it drift away, acknowledging it without engaging. How does this change your perspective on the thought?

Metaphor

The Clouds – Thoughts are like clouds passing through the sky. They come and go, but your true self remains constant beneath them. Allow the clouds to float by without needing to hold onto them.

June 5: Commitment

Quote

"The future depends on what you do today." – *Mahatma Gandhi*

Insight

Committed actions aligned with your values create the future you desire. By taking consistent steps, you build momentum towards your goals and aspirations.

Task

Identify a goal you want to achieve. Outline three specific actions you can take this week to work towards that goal. Commit to taking at least one action each day.

Metaphor

The Brick Wall – Each action you take is like laying a brick in a wall. With each brick, you create a strong structure that supports your future achievements.

June 6: Stress

Quote

"It's not the load that breaks you down, it's the way you carry it." – *Lou Holtz*

Insight

How you perceive and manage stress greatly impacts your wellbeing. Practising acceptance and mindfulness can help you carry life's burdens with more ease.

Task

Identify a stressor in your life. Practise a stress-reducing technique, such as deep breathing or mindfulness, for ten minutes today. Notice how it shifts your perspective.

Metaphor

The Backpack – Imagine your stressors as rocks in a backpack. When you acknowledge and lighten your load through acceptance, you can walk with greater ease and freedom.

June 7: Apathy

Quote

"The only way to do great work is to love what you do." – *Steve Jobs*

Insight

Apathy can stem from disconnecting from your passions and values. Reconnecting with what truly matters to you can reignite motivation and enthusiasm for life.

Task

List three activities that you genuinely enjoy or are passionate about. Make a plan to engage in one of these activities this week. How does it feel to reconnect with what you love?

Metaphor

The Flame – Your passions are like a flame that requires fuel to keep burning. Engage with what inspires you to rekindle your enthusiasm and motivation.

June 8: Growth

Quote

"What lies behind us and what lies before us are tiny matters compared to what lies within us." – *Ralph Waldo Emerson*

Insight

Growth often involves stepping outside your comfort zone and embracing new challenges. By nurturing your inner resources, you can overcome obstacles and flourish.

Task

Reflect on a recent challenge you faced. What did you learn about yourself through this experience? How can you apply this learning to future challenges?

Metaphor

The Caterpillar – A caterpillar must go through a transformation to become a butterfly. Embrace the challenges of growth as necessary steps towards your own transformation.

June 9: Anger

Quote

"Holding onto anger is like drinking poison and expecting the other person to die." – *Buddha*

Insight

Anger can be a heavy burden. Acceptance allows you to acknowledge your anger without being consumed by it, enabling you to respond to situations more mindfully.

Task

When you feel anger today, take a moment to pause. Practise deep breathing and observe the sensations in your body. How does this practice help you process your anger?

Metaphor

The Pressure Cooker – Anger is like a pressure cooker. If not released, it can build up until it explodes. Practising acceptance helps you safely release the pressure.

June 10: Commitment

Quote

"Success is the sum of small efforts, repeated day in and day out." – *Robert Collier*

Insight

Committed actions are the building blocks of success. By focusing on small, daily efforts, you create a strong foundation for achieving your larger goals.

Task

Choose one small goal you want to achieve this month. Break it down into daily actions, and commit to following through on these actions each day.

Metaphor

The Building Blocks – Every small action you take is like adding a block to a tower. Over time, these blocks stack up to create something strong and impressive.

June 11: Acceptance

Quote

"When you accept what is, you are free." – *Byron Katie*

Insight

Acceptance does not mean resignation; it means acknowledging reality. By accepting your circumstances, you open yourself up to new possibilities and choices.

Task

Identify an aspect of your life that you are resisting. Practise acceptance by acknowledging it as it is. What new choices does this perspective open for you?

Metaphor

The Open Door – Acceptance is like opening a door to a new room. Once you let go of resistance, you can explore new possibilities that were previously hidden from view.

June 12: Stress

Quote

"Stress is caused by being 'here' but wanting to be 'there.'" – *Unknown*

Insight

Understanding the roots of your stress can help you manage it better. Practising present moment awareness allows you to appreciate where you are right now, reducing feelings of overwhelm.

Task

Take a moment to breathe deeply and focus on your current surroundings. What do you notice? Practising mindfulness today can help ground you amidst stressors.

Metaphor

The Anchor – In turbulent waters, an anchor stabilises a ship. Your mindfulness practice can serve as an anchor, helping you stay grounded amid life's storms.

June 13: Apathy

Quote

"The only limit to our realisation of tomorrow will be our doubts of today." – *Franklin D. Roosevelt*

Insight

Apathy can often stem from fear of failure. Embracing your fears can open the door to renewed passion and motivation for life.

Task

Identify one fear that has contributed to your apathy. Write down steps you can take to face this fear. What is one small action you can take today?

Metaphor

The Key – Facing your fears is like finding the key to a locked door. Once you unlock it, you open up new opportunities and experiences.

June 14: Values

Quote

"The most powerful thing you can do is to find your own truth." – *Unknown*

Insight

Staying connected to your values empowers you to live authentically. When you honour your true self, you attract opportunities that align with your desires.

Task

Reflect on how your current life aligns with your values. What is one change you can make today to live more authentically?

Metaphor

The North Star – Your values act as your North Star, guiding you through the vastness of life. When you follow them, you navigate with purpose and direction.

June 15: Defusion

Quote

"Thoughts are just thoughts. They don't define you." – *Unknown*

Insight

Learning to defuse from your thoughts empowers you to take control of your reactions. By observing thoughts without attachment, you create space for more thoughtful responses.

Task

Practice a defusion technique today. Whenever a difficult thought arises, repeat it in a silly voice or imagine it on a cloud. Notice how this affects your emotional response.

Metaphor

The Movie Screen – Your thoughts are like a movie playing on a screen. You are the audience, not the characters. By stepping back, you can choose how to engage with the story.

June 16: Committed Action

Quote

"Act as if what you do makes a difference. It does." – *William James*

Insight

Your actions shape your reality. By taking committed steps towards your goals, you create the life you envision for yourself.

Task

Identify a cause or passion that resonates with you. Commit to taking one action this week to support it. How does this commitment make you feel?

Metaphor

The Tapestry – Each action you take is like weaving a thread into a tapestry. Together, they create a beautiful and intricate picture of your life.

June 17

Quote

"The greatest weapon against stress is our ability to choose one thought over another." – *William James*

Insight

Defusion teaches you to separate yourself from stressful thoughts. By recognising that you are not your thoughts, you gain the freedom to choose how you respond to stress, rather than being overwhelmed by it.

Task

Notice one stressful thought you have today. Practise defusion by silently saying, "I am having the thought that..." before repeating the thought. This will create some distance between you and the thought.

Metaphor

Leaves on a Stream – Imagine your stressful thoughts as leaves floating on a stream. You don't have to grab or hold onto them—simply observe as they drift by.

June 18

Quote

"When we are no longer able to change a situation, we are challenged to change ourselves." – *Viktor Frankl*

Insight

Acceptance means letting go of the need to control external situations and focusing instead on how you respond to them. By shifting your attention inward, you can find new strengths and ways to adapt.

Task

Reflect on a situation in your life that you can't control. How might accepting this reality free up energy to focus on what you can change—your thoughts, actions, or reactions?

Metaphor

The Sailboat – You can't control the wind, but you can adjust your sails. Similarly, acceptance helps you adapt to life's changes by adjusting how you respond to them.

June 19

Quote

"The present moment is the only time over which we have dominion." – *Thích Nhất Hạnh*

Insight

Present-moment awareness is about taking control of the only time you truly have: now. By focusing on this moment, you can act with clarity and purpose, instead of being distracted by the past or future.

Task

Spend five minutes today doing a mindfulness exercise. Focus entirely on your breath, the rise and fall of your chest, and the sensations in your body. Allow this to centre you in the present.

Metaphor

The Spotlight – Your attention is like a spotlight. By focusing it on the present moment, you illuminate your path and make conscious choices, rather than stumbling in the dark.

June 20

Quote

"It is not the mountain we conquer but ourselves." – *Edmund Hillary*

Insight

Self-as-context reminds you that no matter the obstacles, it is your internal journey that matters most. Your greatest challenge is mastering your inner world—your thoughts, emotions, and actions.

Task

Think of a recent challenge. What internal qualities—such as courage, persistence, or adaptability—helped you face it? How can you continue to cultivate these qualities?

Metaphor

The Mountain and the Climber – Life's challenges are like mountains. While reaching the summit is important, it's the transformation within the climber that matters most.

June 21: ADHD

Quote

"The secret of getting ahead is getting started." – *Mark Twain*

Insight

For those with ADHD, starting tasks can be a significant barrier. By focusing on just starting, even if it's a small step, you create momentum that can carry you forward.

Task

Pick a task you've been procrastinating on. Set a timer for five minutes and commit to just starting. Once the timer ends, decide if you want to continue or take a break. The key is to begin.

Metaphor

The Snowball – Starting can feel small, like a snowball, but as you keep rolling, it gains momentum and size. Just starting can create the momentum to keep going.

June 22

Quote

"There is no failure except in no longer trying." – *Elbert Hubbard*

Insight

Committed action is about persistence. It's not about achieving perfection but about staying true to your values, even when things get tough. Every small step counts toward meaningful progress.

Task

Identify one area where you've been feeling stuck or discouraged. Commit to taking one small value-driven action today, even if it feels insignificant. Celebrate the act of trying.

Metaphor

The Bricklayer – Building a meaningful life is like laying bricks. Each small action may seem minor on its own, but over time, it creates something strong and lasting.

June 23

Quote

"Happiness is not something ready-made. It comes from your own actions." – *Dalai Lama*

Insight

Happiness and success come from taking action aligned with your values. When you live according to what matters most to you, the result is a deep sense of satisfaction and fulfilment.

Task

Think of one area in your life where you've been seeking happiness. How can you take value-driven action today to create more of that joy for yourself?

Metaphor

The Gardener – Just as a gardener nurtures plants to grow, you create happiness by tending to your values and taking small, daily actions aligned with them.

June 24

Quote

"Don't let yesterday take up too much of today." – *Will Rogers*

Insight

Present-moment awareness reminds you that the past is over, and today is the only time you have. By focusing on the present, you free yourself from the weight of past regrets and make space for new opportunities.

Task

Notice moments today when your mind drifts to the past. Gently guide your attention back to the present by focusing on your breath or surroundings.

Metaphor

The Fresh Canvas – Each day is like a fresh canvas, free from the marks of yesterday. You can choose what to paint today without being restricted by the past.

June 25

Quote

"Life isn't about waiting for the storm to pass; it's about learning to dance in the rain." – *Vivian Greene*

Insight

Acceptance doesn't mean tolerating difficulties passively. It's about engaging with life fully, even when things aren't perfect, and finding joy amidst the challenges.

Task

Think of a current challenge in your life. What value-driven action can you take today to "dance in the rain," embracing the challenge rather than waiting for it to end?

Metaphor

The Dancer – Life's storms are like a dance. Instead of resisting the rain, you can learn to move gracefully through it, finding rhythm and flow even in difficult moments.

June 26: Addiction

Quote

"It always seems impossible until it's done." – *Nelson Mandela*

Insight

Recovery from addiction is a journey of small, committed steps. It may feel overwhelming at times, but with each small action aligned with your values, you are creating a new reality for yourself.

Task

Identify one small action you can take today that aligns with your recovery. Focus on the step ahead, not the entire journey.

Metaphor

The Ladder – Recovery is like climbing a ladder. Each rung brings you higher, and no matter how far you've climbed, the next rung is always within reach. Focus on one step at a time.

June 27: Acceptance

Quote

"Acceptance doesn't mean resignation; it means understanding that something is what it is and that there's got to be a way through it." – *Michael J. Fox*

Insight

Acceptance is a powerful tool that allows you to face reality without denial. By embracing your circumstances, you can explore paths forward rather than feeling trapped by them.

Task

Identify a situation in your life that you have been resisting. Write down three positive outcomes that could come from accepting it as it is. How can this shift your perspective?

Metaphor

The River – Just as a river flows around obstacles rather than resisting them, acceptance allows you to navigate life's challenges with grace and adaptability.

June 28: Stress

Quote

"It's not the stress that kills us, it's our reaction to it." – *Hans Selye*

Insight

Your reaction to stress can amplify or diminish its effects. Practising mindfulness and acceptance can help you respond more effectively to stressors, promoting resilience.

Task

Choose a stress management technique (e.g., deep breathing, yoga, or meditation) and dedicate time to it today. Notice how it impacts your stress levels and overall wellbeing.

Metaphor

The Pressure Valve – Managing stress is like adjusting the pressure valve on a steam cooker. By releasing steam regularly, you prevent an explosion of pressure.

June 29: Committed Action

Quote

"Success is the progressive realisation of a worthy goal or ideal." – *Earl Nightingale*

Insight

Committing to your goals means taking consistent actions, no matter how small. Every step you take contributes to your overall journey towards success.

Task

Reflect on a long-term goal you have. Write down three small steps you can take today to move closer to achieving it. Commit to one of these actions before the end of the day.

Metaphor

The Mountain Climber – Climbing a mountain requires perseverance and commitment. Each step up brings you closer to the summit, no matter how challenging the climb may be.

June 30: Values

Quote

"Your life is a reflection of your values. Choose wisely." – *Unknown*

Insight

Your values shape your choices and ultimately the life you lead. By living in accordance with your values, you create a more fulfilling and authentic life.

Task

Take time to revisit your list of values. Choose one value to focus on for the upcoming month. How can you ensure your actions reflect this value daily?

Metaphor

The Lighthouse – Your values serve as a lighthouse, guiding you through life's storms. When you stay true to them, you can navigate safely towards your destination.

JULY

July 1: Present Moment Awareness

Quote

"The only thing that ever matters is this moment." – *Unknown*

Insight

Living in the present moment allows you to fully experience life as it unfolds. By focusing on the here and now, you can cultivate gratitude and joy in everyday experiences.

Task

Set a timer for five minutes. During this time, focus on your breath and observe any sensations or sounds around you. What do you notice that you might usually overlook?

Metaphor

The Movie Reel – Life is like a movie reel; each frame represents a moment. By paying attention to each frame, you can appreciate the beauty of the entire film.

July 2: Acceptance

Quote

"The first step toward change is awareness. The second step is acceptance." – *Nathaniel Branden*

Insight

Acceptance is about recognising your current reality without judgement. It opens the door to change and growth, allowing you to respond more effectively to life's challenges.

Task

Reflect on a recent disappointment. Write down how accepting this situation could lead to new opportunities or insights. How can you practise acceptance today?

Metaphor

The Flower – Just as a flower blooms by accepting the conditions it is given, you too can flourish by accepting where you are in life.

July 3: Values

Quote

"Values are like fingerprints. Nobody's are the same, but you leave 'em all over everything you do." – *Elvis Presley*

Insight

Your values guide your decisions and actions. Understanding them helps you live authentically, creating a sense of direction and purpose in your life.

Task

Write down three values that resonate deeply with you. Reflect on how your actions align with these values. What is one step you can take this week to live more in accordance with your values?

Metaphor

The Road Map – Your values act as a road map, guiding you through life's journey. When you know where you want to go, you can choose the best path to get there.

July 4: Defusion

Quote

"You are not a drop in the ocean. You are the entire ocean in a drop." – *Rumi*

Insight

Defusion helps you detach from unhelpful thoughts, enabling you to see them for what they are—just thoughts. This perspective frees you to act in alignment with your values.

Task

Choose a negative thought that often resurfaces. Write it down and then repeat it out loud in a funny voice. Notice how this changes your relationship with the thought.

Metaphor

The Glass of Water – Your thoughts are like a glass of water; they can be clear or muddy. By practising defusion, you can clear the murkiness and see the truth beneath.

July 5: Committed Action

Quote

"Action is the foundational key to all success." – *Pablo Picasso*

Insight

Committing to action is essential for progress. Small, consistent steps taken towards your goals can create significant change over time.

Task

Identify a long-term goal you want to achieve. Break it down into smaller, actionable steps. Choose one step to focus on today and commit to completing it.

Metaphor

The Garden – Just as a garden flourishes with regular care, your goals thrive with consistent action. Tend to your aspirations daily for them to blossom.

July 6: Stress

Quote

"Stress is an indicator, not a curse." – *Unknown*

Insight

Recognising the sources of your stress can empower you to manage it effectively. Viewing stress as a signal can help you identify areas of your life that need attention.

Task

Take a moment to list your current stressors. Choose one to focus on and develop a plan to address it. How can you take proactive steps to alleviate this stress?

Metaphor

The Alarm Bell – Stress acts as an alarm bell, alerting you to areas of your life needing attention. Listen to its message and take action to restore balance.

July 7: Apathy

Quote

"The opposite of love is not hate; it's indifference." – *Elie Wiesel*

Insight

Apathy can sap your energy and motivation. Reconnecting with your values and passions can reignite your enthusiasm for life.

Task

Write down three things you are passionate about or enjoy doing. Make a plan to engage in one of these activities this week. How does this affect your sense of motivation?

Metaphor

The Spark – Your passions are like sparks that ignite your enthusiasm. Nurturing them can light the fire within, driving you towards action.

July 8: Growth

Quote

"The only way to grow is to face your fears." – *Unknown*

Insight

Embracing challenges is essential for personal growth. Each experience, whether positive or negative, offers opportunities to learn and evolve.

Task

Identify a fear that has held you back. Write down steps you can take to face this fear, starting with a small action you can take today.

Metaphor

The Phoenix – Just as a phoenix rises from its ashes, facing your fears can lead to rebirth and growth, transforming you into a stronger version of yourself.

July 9: Values

Quote

"To live is the rarest thing in the world. Most people exist, that is all." – *Oscar Wilde*

Insight

Living in alignment with your values allows you to truly experience life. When you connect with what matters most, you enrich your existence.

Task

Reflect on a value that is important to you. How can you incorporate it into your daily life? Make a plan to honour this value today.

Metaphor

The Canvas – Your life is a canvas, and your values are the colours. By choosing to live authentically, you create a masterpiece unique to you.

July 10: Defusion

Quote

"Thoughts are not facts." – *Unknown*

Insight

Learning to view your thoughts as just thoughts rather than absolute truths allows you to respond to them with more freedom and choice.

Task

Practice a defusion technique today. For example, try visualising a troublesome thought as a cloud floating away. How does this change your perception of the thought?

Metaphor

The Train – Your thoughts are like trains passing through a station. You can choose whether to board them or let them pass by without getting on.

July 11: Committed Action

Quote

"The journey of a thousand miles begins with one step." – *Lao Tzu*

Insight

Every small step taken towards your goals adds up to significant progress. Committing to consistent actions can lead you to where you want to be.

Task

Choose a goal you want to achieve. Write down three small, actionable steps you can take this week to move closer to that goal. Commit to taking at least one step each day.

Metaphor

The Staircase – Achieving your goals is like climbing a staircase. Each step brings you closer to the top, and every step counts, no matter how small.

July 12: Anger

Quote

"Anger is a wind which blows out the lamp of the mind." – *Robert Green Ingersoll*

Insight

Understanding your anger can help you manage it more effectively. Rather than letting anger control you, explore its roots to find healthier ways to respond.

Task

Reflect on a recent situation that made you angry. Write down what triggered your anger and how you could respond differently in the future.

Metaphor

The Volcano – Anger is like a volcano; if left unchecked, it can erupt. By acknowledging it and finding healthy outlets, you can prevent an explosion.

July 13: Apathy

Quote

"The only way to do great work is to love what you do." – *Steve Jobs*

Insight

Apathy can arise from a lack of passion in your work or life. Discovering what you truly enjoy can rekindle your motivation and energy.

Task

List three activities that make you feel alive. Choose one to engage in today, focusing on the joy it brings you.

Metaphor

The Flame – Your passions are like a flame that can warm your soul. Feed them to keep the fire alive and avoid the cold of apathy.

July 14: Stress

Quote

"Almost everything will work again if you unplug it for a few minutes, including you." – *Anne Lamott*

Insight

Taking breaks and allowing yourself to recharge is essential for managing stress. Stepping back can give you a fresh perspective and renewed energy.

Task

Schedule a short break during your day to do something enjoyable, like going for a walk or reading a book. Notice how it affects your stress levels.

Metaphor

The Battery – Just as a battery needs recharging, so do you. Make time for self-care to ensure you stay energised and resilient.

July 15: Acceptance

Quote

"What you resist, persists." – *Carl Jung*

Insight

Acceptance can help you break free from the cycle of resistance. Embracing reality allows you to move forward rather than remain stuck in frustration.

Task

Identify something you've been resisting. Write down three ways acceptance could help you move forward in this situation. How can you begin to practise acceptance today?

Metaphor

The Leaf on the Water – Accepting your circumstances is like letting a leaf float on water; it can move freely without fighting against the current.

July 16: Values

Quote

"Live your values. You'll be happier, and so will the world." – *Unknown*

Insight

Aligning your actions with your values leads to a more fulfilling and meaningful life. Living authentically is a gift you give to yourself and those around you.

Task

Choose one value to focus on today. Find ways to incorporate it into your interactions or decisions. Notice how it influences your mood and sense of purpose.

Metaphor

The Compass – Your values act as a compass, guiding you through life. When you stay true to them, you navigate with clarity and purpose.

July 17: Committed Action

Quote

"You don't have to be great to start, but you have to start to be great." – *Zig Ziglar*

Insight

Taking action, regardless of its size, is the key to making progress. Every effort counts, and starting is often the most challenging yet rewarding step.

Task

Identify a goal you've been hesitant to pursue. Write down one small action you can take today to start moving towards it. Commit to doing it.

Metaphor

The Seed – A seed needs to be planted to grow. Taking that first step is like planting the seed of your ambitions, allowing them to flourish over time.

July 18: Anger

Quote

"For every minute you are angry, you lose sixty seconds of happiness." – *Ralph Waldo Emerson*

Insight

Anger can steal your joy and prevent you from experiencing the present moment. Learning to manage your anger can free you to embrace happiness and peace.

Task

When you feel anger rising today, pause and take three deep breaths. Notice how this simple action affects your emotional state and allows you to respond more thoughtfully.

Metaphor

The Traffic Light – Your emotions are like traffic lights. Recognising anger as a red light gives you the opportunity to stop, breathe, and choose your response.

July 19: Apathy

Quote

"The greatest danger for most of us is not that our aim is too high and we miss it, but that it is too low and we reach it." – *Michelangelo*

Insight

Apathy often stems from setting unchallenging goals. Challenging yourself can reignite your passion and motivation, helping you live a more fulfilling life.

Task

Reflect on your current goals. Are they inspiring enough? Set a new, more ambitious goal that excites you. Write down the first steps you will take to pursue it.

Metaphor

The Climbing Wall – Life's challenges are like climbing a wall; the higher you climb, the more rewarding the view. Push yourself to reach new heights.

July 20: Present Moment Awareness

Quote

"Wherever you are, be all there." – *Jim Elliot*

Insight

Being fully present allows you to engage deeply with life. This awareness fosters richer experiences and connections with others.

Task

Throughout the day, practice being fully present in your interactions. Put away distractions and give your complete attention to those around you.

Metaphor

The Spotlight – Imagine a spotlight shining on the present moment. By focusing your attention here, you illuminate the richness of your experiences.

July 21: Defusion

Quote

"You are not your thoughts." – *Unknown*

Insight

Understanding that your thoughts do not define you allows you to detach from negativity. This perspective empowers you to take action in line with your values.

Task

Choose a negative thought that often comes to mind. Write it down, and then write a counter-statement that reflects your values. Reflect on this new perspective.

Metaphor

The Bubble – Imagine your thoughts as bubbles floating away. By practising defusion, you can let go of the ones that weigh you down.

July 22: Acceptance

Quote

"Sometimes the bravest and most important thing you can do is just show up." – *Brene Brown*

Insight

Acceptance means facing your feelings and situations without avoidance. Showing up for yourself is a courageous step towards healing and growth.

Task

Take a moment to acknowledge your feelings today, even the uncomfortable ones. Write them down and reflect on how accepting them can help you move forward.

Metaphor

The Open Door – Acceptance is like opening a door to new possibilities. By allowing yourself to feel and experience, you create space for growth and healing.

July 23: Values

Quote

"It is not enough to be busy; so are the ants. The question is: What are we busy about?" – *Henry David Thoreau*

Insight

Being busy does not equate to being fulfilled. Aligning your daily activities with your values ensures that your busyness is meaningful.

Task

Today, assess how you spend your time. Are your activities aligned with your values? Identify one change you can make to ensure your time reflects what truly matters to you.

Metaphor

The Balancing Act – Life is a balancing act. By prioritising your values, you can ensure that your time is spent on what truly matters, creating a harmonious life.

July 24: Committed Action

Quote

"Success usually comes to those who are too busy to be looking for it." – *Henry David Thoreau*

Insight

Committing to action often leads to success. When you focus on your goals and take consistent steps, you attract opportunities and progress.

Task

Think about a long-term goal. Write down three specific actions you can take this week to move closer to achieving it. Choose one to focus on today.

Metaphor

The Train Tracks – Your actions are like train tracks leading you toward your destination. Stay on course, and you will reach your goals.

July 25: Anger

Quote

"Holding onto anger is like drinking poison and expecting the other person to die." – *Buddha*

Insight

Letting go of anger is essential for your wellbeing. Recognising that holding onto it harms you more than others can help you find peace.

Task

Identify a source of anger in your life. Write a letter expressing your feelings, but do not send it. Reflect on how releasing these emotions impacts you.

Metaphor

The Balloon – Letting go of anger is like releasing a balloon; it lifts you up and frees you from the weight of negativity.

July 26: Apathy

Quote

"If you want to conquer fear, don't sit home and think about it. Go out and get busy." – *Dale Carnegie*

Insight

Apathy can be countered by taking action. Engaging in activities that challenge you can reignite your motivation and passion.

Task

Identify an area of your life where you feel apathetic. Choose a small, bold action to take today that can help you break out of this state.

Metaphor

The Wave – Apathy is like a wave that can pull you under. By taking action, you can swim back to the surface and regain control.

July 27: Present Moment Awareness

Quote

"The mind is everything. What you think you become." – *Buddha*

Insight

Your thoughts shape your reality. Cultivating present moment awareness helps you focus on the positive aspects of your life and what truly matters.

Task

Spend five minutes today observing your surroundings without judgement. Notice details you may have overlooked before. How does this practice shift your perspective?

Metaphor

The Magnifying Glass – Awareness acts as a magnifying glass, bringing clarity to the present moment and revealing the beauty that surrounds you.

July 28: Defusion

Quote

"Thoughts are just thoughts; they can come and go like clouds in the sky." – *Unknown*

Insight

Defusion involves observing your thoughts without getting entangled in them. This practice allows you to create space and distance from negative thinking.

Task

Identify a recurring negative thought today. Write it down and then practice defusion by repeating it out loud, observing how it feels detached from your identity.

Metaphor

The Cloud – Your thoughts are like clouds in the sky; they may block the sun temporarily, but they will eventually pass. Allow them to drift by without judgement.

July 29: Acceptance

Quote

"Sometimes the most productive thing you can do is rest and relax." – *Unknown*

Insight

Acceptance is not about resignation but acknowledging your reality. It's okay to rest and allow yourself to feel without the pressure to change immediately.

Task

Take a moment to sit quietly and acknowledge any feelings you have been resisting. Write them down, recognising that it's okay to feel what you feel.

Metaphor

The River – Acceptance is like a river flowing; it moves through obstacles without resistance. Allow your feelings to flow freely, guiding you toward understanding.

July 30: Values

Quote

"Your values create your actions, and your actions create your life." – *Unknown*

Insight

Understanding your core values can help you make choices that lead to a fulfilling life. Live according to your values, and you'll find more joy and satisfaction.

Task

Reflect on a decision you made recently. How did your values influence that choice? Write down how you can ensure future decisions align with your values.

Metaphor

The Garden – Your values are like seeds in a garden. Nurture them, and they will grow into a vibrant and meaningful life.

July 31: Committed Action

Quote

"You cannot swim for new horizons until you have courage to lose sight of the shore." – *William Faulkner*

Insight

Committed action often requires stepping outside your comfort zone. Embracing uncertainty can lead to new opportunities and personal growth.

Task

Identify an area where you feel comfortable but limited. Write down one action you can take this week that challenges you to step outside that comfort zone.

Metaphor

The Ocean – Committing to action is like sailing into the vast ocean. While it may feel daunting, the journey can lead to uncharted and rewarding territories.

AUGUST

August 1: Acceptance

Quote

"The first step toward change is awareness. The second step is acceptance." – *Nathaniel Branden*

Insight

Acceptance allows us to confront our feelings and circumstances honestly. By acknowledging what is, we empower ourselves to make informed changes.

Task

Take a moment today to reflect on something you have been resisting. Write it down, acknowledging your feelings about it without judgement.

Metaphor

The Mirror – Acceptance is like looking in a mirror; it reflects reality. By facing it, you can better understand yourself and the changes you wish to make.

August 2: Values

Quote

"Your time is limited, don't waste it living someone else's life." – *Steve Jobs*

Insight

Living according to your values ensures that your life reflects your true self. This alignment fosters happiness and fulfilment.

Task

List your top three values. For each, write down one specific way you can express these values in your daily life starting today.

Metaphor

The North Star – Your values are your North Star, guiding you through the night sky of life. Stay true to them, and you will find your way.

August 3: Present Moment Awareness

Quote

"The only way to experience life is to live it." – *Unknown*

Insight

Being present allows you to fully engage with life's moments. Mindfulness enhances your experiences and relationships.

Task

Set aside five minutes today to sit quietly. Focus on your breath and notice the sensations in your body. Allow thoughts to come and go without judgement.

Metaphor

The Stopwatch – Present moment awareness is like a stopwatch; it encourages you to pause and fully experience the 'now' rather than racing ahead.

August 4: Defusion

Quote

"You are not a drop in the ocean. You are the entire ocean in a drop." – *Rumi*

Insight

Defusion helps create distance from your thoughts, allowing you to see them as separate from your identity. This practice can help you manage negative thinking.

Task

Choose a negative thought you often experience. Write it down, then rephrase it as a simple statement without emotional charge. Notice how it feels.

Metaphor

The Train on the Track – Your thoughts are like trains on a track. You can choose to let them pass by without boarding them.

August 5: Committed Action

Quote

"The journey of a thousand miles begins with one step." – *Lao Tzu*

Insight

Taking committed action, no matter how small, propels you toward your goals. Each step you take builds momentum and confidence.

Task

Identify a goal you have been postponing. Write down one action you can take today, no matter how small, to move towards that goal.

Metaphor

The Staircase – Every action is a step on a staircase. Take that first step, and each subsequent step will feel more attainable.

August 6: Stress

Quote

"Stress is caused by being 'here' but wanting to be 'there.'" – *Eckhart Tolle*

Insight

Recognising where your stress comes from can help you manage it. Often, it stems from our desire for things to be different than they are.

Task

Today, notice when you feel stressed. Write down the situation and explore what you are resisting. How can acceptance ease this stress?

Metaphor

The Tension Rod – Stress is like a tension rod being pulled tight. Acknowledging your feelings can relieve that tension and restore balance.

August 7: Anger

Quote

"To be angry is to let others' mistakes teach you a lesson." – *Anger Management Proverb*

Insight

Anger often arises from feeling wronged. Understanding its triggers can help you respond more constructively and avoid holding onto resentment.

Task

Think of a time you felt anger towards someone. Write down what triggered that anger and how you could communicate your feelings more openly.

Metaphor

The Caged Bird – Anger can feel like a caged bird; it wants to fly but is trapped. Finding healthy outlets allows it to soar.

August 8: Apathy

Quote

"The opposite of love is not hate; it's indifference." – *Elie Wiesel*

Insight

Apathy can be a sign of disconnection from your passions. Reconnecting with what you love can reignite your motivation and purpose.

Task

List three things that once excited you but you have stopped doing. Choose one to re-engage with today and notice how it makes you feel.

Metaphor

The Dormant Seed – Apathy is like a seed lying dormant. Nurturing your passions allows them to sprout and flourish.

August 9: Present Moment Awareness

Quote

"Be here now." – *Ram Dass*

Insight

Practising present moment awareness brings you back to what is important. It allows you to fully engage with your life and cultivate appreciation for the here and now.

Task

Throughout your day, set reminders to pause and take three deep breaths. Observe your surroundings, and engage your senses fully.

Metaphor

The Photograph – Present moment awareness is like taking a snapshot of life. It captures the beauty of the moment, allowing you to savour it.

August 10: Defusion

Quote

"You are the sky. Everything else – it's just the weather." – *Pema Chödrön*

Insight

Defusion allows you to see your thoughts as transient. Understanding that they come and go can help reduce their impact on your emotions and actions.

Task

Today, practice defusion by observing your thoughts as if they were leaves floating down a stream. Notice how this practice changes your emotional landscape.

Metaphor

The Passing Train – Your thoughts are like trains passing through a station. You can choose which ones to board and which to let go.

August 11: Committed Action

Quote

"Action is the foundational key to all success." – *Pablo Picasso*

Insight

Committed action is essential for progress. Making a conscious decision to act helps you move closer to your goals, one step at a time.

Task

Identify a long-term goal. Write down three specific actions you can take this month to advance towards it, and commit to starting one today.

Metaphor

The Building Block – Each action is a building block in the structure of your dreams. Lay them down carefully to create a solid foundation.

August 12: Stress

Quote

"Stress is not what happens to us. It's our response to what happens. And response is something we can choose." – *Viktor E. Frankl*

Insight

How you respond to stress is within your control. Practising mindfulness can help you cultivate a more balanced and resilient approach to life's challenges.

Task

When you feel stressed today, pause and take three deep breaths. Notice how this simple act shifts your perspective and calms your mind.

August 13: Anger

Quote

"Holding onto anger is like drinking poison and expecting the other person to die." – *Buddha*

Insight

Letting go of anger frees you from its burden. Acknowledging your feelings and finding constructive ways to express them is essential for emotional health.

Task

Write a letter expressing your anger about a situation, but do not send it. Allow yourself to vent your feelings, then reflect on how to communicate constructively.

Metaphor

The Balloon – Anger can inflate like a balloon. Releasing your feelings safely can help deflate that balloon, restoring peace.

August 14: Apathy

Quote

"People are just as happy as they make up their minds to be."
– *Abraham Lincoln*

Insight

Apathy can be overcome by actively choosing engagement in your life. Small steps towards things you care about can reignite your passion and enthusiasm.

Task

Identify one area in your life where you feel apathetic. Choose a small action you can take today to engage with it differently.

Metaphor

The Flickering Flame – Apathy is like a flickering flame; it needs air to burn bright. Feed your interests to keep the flame alive.

August 15: Present Moment Awareness

Quote

"Wherever you are, be all there." – *Jim Elliot*

Insight

Fully engaging with the present allows you to experience life more richly. Mindfulness fosters deeper connections and enhances overall well-being.

Task

Today, focus on one task at a time. Notice your thoughts and feelings during the task, and let distractions drift away.

Metaphor

The Spotlight – Being present is like shining a spotlight on the moment, illuminating your experiences and allowing them to unfold in their full richness.

August 16: Committed Action

Quote

"Success is not the key to happiness. Happiness is the key to success. If you love what you are doing, you will be successful." – *Albert Schweitzer*

Insight

Committed action driven by passion leads to success. When you align your actions with what you love, you create a fulfilling and meaningful life.

Task

Reflect on your current commitments. Are they aligned with your passions? Write down one change you can make to better align your actions with your interests.

Metaphor

The Riverbank – Your passions are like the riverbank guiding the flow of water. Let them shape your path as you move forward.

August 17: Acceptance

Quote

"Acceptance doesn't mean resignation; it means understanding that something is what it is and that there's got to be a way through it." – *Michael J. Fox*

Insight

Acceptance opens the door to change. When you accept your reality, you can identify actionable steps to navigate through it.

Task

Identify a situation you're struggling with. Write down three ways you can accept this situation and one small action you can take towards improvement.

Metaphor

The Bridge – Acceptance is a bridge over troubled waters, helping you cross from where you are to where you want to be.

August 18: Defusion

Quote

"Thoughts are not facts." – *Unknown*

Insight

Understanding that your thoughts are just thoughts helps reduce their power over you. Defusion techniques allow you to create space between you and your thoughts.

Task

Today, choose a thought that bothers you and write it on a piece of paper. Then, read it in a silly voice or a funny accent. Notice how this alters your perception of it.

Metaphor

The Playful Child – Think of your thoughts as a playful child. You don't have to take every action they suggest; you can choose to play along or set them aside.

August 19: Values

Quote

"Act as if what you do makes a difference. It does." – *William James*

Insight

Your actions grounded in your values create ripples that affect not just your life but the lives of those around you. Your choices matter.

Task

Choose one value to embody today. Identify one way you can reflect this value in your interactions and commit to it.

Metaphor

The Ripple Effect – Just as a stone creates ripples in a pond, your actions grounded in values can inspire others and create positive change.

August 20: Present Moment Awareness

Quote

"The mind is a wonderful servant but a terrible master." – *David Allen*

Insight

When you practice present moment awareness, you learn to manage your thoughts instead of being controlled by them. Mindfulness empowers you.

Task

Throughout the day, set a timer for every hour. When it goes off, take a moment to check in with yourself. How are you feeling? What are you thinking? What can you notice around you?

Metaphor

The Anchor – Present moment awareness is like an anchor, keeping you grounded in the tumultuous seas of thoughts and distractions.

August 21: Stress

Quote

"It's not the load that breaks you down, it's the way you carry it." – *Lou Holtz*

Insight

Your perspective on stress can change your experience of it. Finding healthy coping mechanisms can transform how you manage stressors.

Task

Identify one stressor in your life. Write down three strategies you can implement to cope with this stress more effectively.

Metaphor

The Backpack – Imagine your stress as a backpack. You can choose what to carry and how to lighten the load by removing unnecessary items.

August 22: Anger

Quote

"For every minute you are angry, you lose sixty seconds of happiness." – *Ralph Waldo Emerson*

Insight

Recognising the cost of anger can motivate you to address it constructively. Embracing healthy communication can lead to resolution and peace.

Task

When you feel anger today, pause and take three deep breaths before reacting. Reflect on the underlying feelings behind your anger and how you can express them calmly.

Metaphor

The Volcano – Anger can build up like pressure in a volcano. Find safe outlets for your emotions to prevent an explosive eruption.

August 23: Apathy

Quote

"The biggest adventure you can take is to live the life of your dreams." – *Oprah Winfrey*

Insight

Reigniting your passions can help overcome apathy. Identify what excites you and take steps to re-engage with those interests.

Task

Choose one hobby or interest that you have neglected. Dedicate at least 30 minutes today to explore or engage with it.

Metaphor

The Blooming Flower – Apathy is like a flower that hasn't bloomed. Nurturing your passions can help you blossom.

August 24: Defusion

Quote

"You don't have to believe everything you think." – *Unknown*

Insight

Defusion techniques can help you detach from unhelpful thoughts. Recognising them as mere mental events can reduce their emotional weight.

Task

Practice defusion by observing a thought you usually take seriously. Write it down, then add "I notice that I'm having the thought that..." before it.

Metaphor

The Balloon Again – Just like letting go of a helium balloon, you can choose to release unhelpful thoughts and allow them to float away.

August 25: Values

Quote

"What you do makes a difference, and you have to decide what kind of difference you want to make." – *Jane Goodall*

Insight

Your values shape the impact you have on the world. By acting in alignment with your values, you contribute to a life of significance.

Task

Choose a value that you wish to express more in your life. Write down three actions you can take this week to embody that value.

Metaphor

The Lighthouse – Your values are like a lighthouse, guiding your actions and illuminating the way for yourself and others.

August 26: Present Moment Awareness

Quote

"The future depends on what you do today." – *Mahatma Gandhi*

Insight

Focusing on the present empowers you to make choices that shape your future. Every moment is an opportunity for growth and change.

Task

Throughout your day, practice mindfulness during routine tasks, such as eating or walking. Notice the sensations and experiences involved in each action.

Metaphor

The Sculptor – Each moment is like a stroke of a sculptor's chisel, shaping the masterpiece of your life. Be present to create a work of art.

August 27: Stress

Quote

"Stress is not a bad thing. It can help us get things done." – *Unknown*

Insight

Understanding stress as a natural part of life can change how you respond to it. Healthy coping strategies can transform stress into motivation.

Task

Identify a recent stressful situation. Reflect on how you can turn that stress into a positive outcome through constructive action.

Metaphor

The Pressure Cooker – Like a pressure cooker, stress can help build pressure for action, but it's essential to release steam safely.

August 28: Anger

Quote

"Anger is a choice. It is a feeling that can be transformed." – *Unknown*

Insight

Recognising that you have the power to manage your anger can empower you to respond more effectively. Choosing to transform anger can lead to healing.

Task

Reflect on a time when you felt anger. What did you learn from that experience? How can you apply that lesson to future situations?

Metaphor

The Phoenix – Just as the phoenix rises from its ashes, you can transform anger into a catalyst for growth and renewal.

August 29: Apathy

Quote

"Life is either a daring adventure or nothing at all." – *Helen Keller*

Insight

Choosing to engage with life as an adventure can counteract feelings of apathy. Seek out new experiences and challenges that excite you.

Task

Plan an adventure for the weekend, no matter how small. It could be exploring a new place or trying a new hobby. Make it an experience that excites you.

Metaphor

The Explorer – Approach life like an explorer discovering new lands. Embrace curiosity and the thrill of the unknown.

August 30: Committed Action

Quote

"The only way to do great work is to love what you do." – *Steve Jobs*

Insight

Committing to your passions is essential for achieving great things. When you love what you do, your actions are energised and meaningful.

Task

Spend time today identifying projects or tasks that excite you. Make a plan to devote time to these passions in the coming weeks.

Metaphor

The Artisan – Your life is a masterpiece in the making. Pour your heart into your craft, and watch your passion transform your work.

August 31: Acceptance

Quote

"The greatest discovery of my generation is that a human being can alter his life by altering his attitudes." – *William James*

Insight

Accepting your current state allows you to alter your future. Shifting your attitude towards acceptance creates space for growth and transformation.

Task

Write down three things you are currently struggling to accept. Reflect on how acceptance could help you move forward with these challenges.

Metaphor

The Open Door – Acceptance is an open door, welcoming new possibilities and experiences as you navigate through life

SEPTEMBER

September 1: Values

Quote

"The most important thing is to enjoy your life—to be happy—it's all that matters." – *Audrey Hepburn*

Insight

Living according to your values brings genuine happiness and fulfilment. Identifying and prioritising your core values can lead to a more meaningful life.

Task

Take a moment to write down your top three values. Reflect on how you can incorporate them into your daily life.

Metaphor

The Compass – Your values are like a compass, guiding you through the journey of life and helping you navigate choices and challenges.

September 2: Acceptance

Quote

"Acceptance is the first step to change." – *Unknown*

Insight

Embracing acceptance creates a foundation for growth. When you accept your current circumstances, you empower yourself to make meaningful changes.

Task

Identify one aspect of your life you find difficult to accept. Write down how accepting this reality might change your approach to it.

Metaphor

The Tree – Acceptance is like a tree with deep roots; it allows you to stand strong through storms while remaining open to new growth.

September 3: Defusion

Quote

"You are not your thoughts." – *Unknown*

Insight

Defusion techniques allow you to separate your identity from your thoughts. This separation can reduce the power of unhelpful thoughts and foster a more positive mindset.

Task

Choose a negative thought you often experience. Write it down, then counter it with a more constructive perspective.

Metaphor

The Clouds – Thoughts are like clouds in the sky; they come and go. You are the sky, vast and unchanged by the passing clouds.

September 4: Present Moment Awareness

Quote

"The present moment is filled with joy and happiness. If you are attentive, you will see it." – *Thich Nhat Hanh*

Insight

Mindfulness cultivates joy and awareness in everyday life. When you focus on the present, you can experience life more fully and appreciate the small things.

Task

Spend five minutes today in silence, focusing on your breath. Notice any sensations or thoughts that arise without judgement.

Metaphor

The Still Pond – Present moment awareness is like a still pond, reflecting the beauty of the world around you, undisturbed by the chaos of thoughts.

September 5: Stress

Quote

"Stress is not what happens to us. It's our response to what happens. And response is something we can choose." – *Viktor Frankl*

Insight

How you respond to stress can transform your experience. By choosing healthier coping mechanisms, you can manage stress more effectively.

Task

Identify a stressor in your life. Write down three constructive ways to manage your response to this stressor moving forward.

Metaphor

The Calm Before the Storm – Just as a calm can exist before a storm, you can find peace amidst the chaos of stress.

September 6: Anger

Quote

"Anger is a wind that blows out the lamp of the mind." – *Robert G. Ingersoll*

Insight

Recognising your anger allows you to channel it positively. Rather than letting it cloud your judgement, use it as a catalyst for change.

Task

When you feel anger rising today, pause and write down what triggered that anger. Reflect on how you might express that feeling constructively.

Metaphor

The Tidal Wave – Anger can surge like a tidal wave. Learning to surf it rather than being swept away can lead to more constructive outcomes.

September 7: Apathy

Quote

"The greatest danger for most of us is not that our aim is too high and we miss it, but that it is too low and we reach it." – *Michelangelo*

Insight

Apathy can stem from setting low expectations. Challenging yourself with higher aims can reignite your passion and motivation.

Task

Set a small but ambitious goal for yourself this week. Write down the steps needed to achieve it and commit to taking action.

Metaphor

The Climbing Mountain – Apathy can be a flat terrain; setting higher goals is like climbing a mountain, providing both challenge and exhilaration.

September 8: Committed Action

Quote

"You miss 100% of the shots you don't take." – *Wayne Gretzky*

Insight

Taking action is crucial for achieving your goals. Committed action, rooted in your values, can lead you to success.

Task

Identify a project you've been putting off. Take one small action today towards making it happen, no matter how minor it seems.

Metaphor

The Seed – Committed action is like planting a seed; it may seem small, but with care and effort, it can grow into something magnificent.

September 9: Values

Quote

"Do not go where the path may lead, go instead where there is no path and leave a trail." – *Ralph Waldo Emerson*

Insight

Your values can inspire you to carve your own path in life. Living authentically encourages others to do the same.

Task

Today, think of someone who embodies values you admire. Reflect on how you can incorporate some of those values into your own life.

Metaphor

The Trailblazer – Like a trailblazer in a forest, following your values can create a path for others to follow, fostering inspiration.

September 10: Acceptance

Quote

"To be yourself in a world that is constantly trying to make you something else is the greatest accomplishment." – *Ralph Waldo Emerson*

Insight

Acceptance of your true self is vital for personal growth. When you embrace who you are, you empower yourself to live authentically.

Task

Write down three qualities that make you unique. How can you celebrate these qualities in your daily life?

Metaphor

The Unique Gem – Acceptance is like recognising the beauty of a gem; each facet has its own worth and contributes to the whole.

September 11: Defusion

Quote

"Thoughts are like clouds—fleeting and transient." – *Unknown*

Insight

Learning to defuse from your thoughts allows you to observe them without being overwhelmed. This perspective fosters clarity and peace.

Task

Practice noticing a thought as it arises. Acknowledge it, then visualise it floating away like a cloud, creating space for clarity.

Metaphor

The Stream – Your thoughts are like leaves floating on a stream. Allow them to pass without clinging or pushing against them.

September 12: Present Moment Awareness

Quote

"Yesterday is history. Tomorrow is a mystery. Today is a gift of God, which is why we call it the present." – *Bill Keane*

Insight

Valuing the present moment allows you to experience life as it unfolds. It is the key to finding joy in everyday experiences.

Task

Take a mindful walk today. Pay attention to your surroundings, the sounds, the colours, and how your body feels as you move.

September 13: Stress

Quote

"It's not the load that breaks you down, it's the way you carry it." – *Lou Holtz*

Insight

How you manage stress makes all the difference. Developing healthy coping strategies can transform burdens into manageable tasks.

Task

List three stressors in your life. Next to each, write down a coping strategy that could help you manage them effectively.

Metaphor

The Backpack – Your stress is like a backpack; if it's too heavy, learn to lighten the load by letting go of what you don't need.

September 14: Anger

Quote

"The best fighter is never angry." – *Lao Tzu*

Insight

Responding to anger with composure is a strength. Learning to manage your reactions can lead to healthier interactions.

Task

When you feel anger bubbling up today, take a deep breath and count to ten before responding. Observe how this impacts your reaction.

Metaphor

The Gentle Stream – Anger can disrupt the flow of life, but a gentle stream moves around obstacles, teaching us to respond with grace.

September 15: Apathy

Quote

"Act as if what you do makes a difference. It does." – *William James*

Insight

Even small actions can combat feelings of apathy. Recognising the impact of your contributions can reignite motivation and engagement.

Task

Today, do something kind for someone else. Notice how this act affects your mood and feelings of engagement.

Metaphor

The Ripple Effect – Your actions can create ripples in the lives of others, spreading positivity and energy beyond what you can see.

September 16: Committed Action

Quote

"The future depends on what you do today." – *Mahatma Gandhi*

Insight

Every small action you take today lays the groundwork for your future. Committing to your goals fosters growth and success.

Task

Identify one long-term goal and break it down into three actionable steps you can take this week.

Metaphor

The Brick Wall – Each action is a brick in the wall of your success. Build it one brick at a time, and it will stand strong.

September 17: Values

Quote

"The ultimate measure of a man is not where he stands in moments of comfort, but where he stands at times of challenge and controversy." – *Martin Luther King Jr.*

Insight

Your values are especially vital during challenging times. They guide your actions and decisions when faced with adversity.

Task

Reflect on a recent challenge. How did your values influence your decisions in that situation? Write down your thoughts.

Metaphor

The Anchor – Your values serve as an anchor in turbulent seas, keeping you grounded amidst the storms of life.

September 18: Acceptance

Quote

"What lies behind us and what lies before us are tiny matters compared to what lies within us." – *Ralph Waldo Emerson*

Insight

Acceptance is an internal process that empowers you to move forward. Embracing who you are and where you are can unlock your potential.

Task

Identify a situation you've been resisting. Write down three positive outcomes that could arise from accepting it.

Metaphor

The River – Acceptance is like a river flowing around obstacles, adapting and continuing on its path rather than resisting the journey.

September 19: Defusion

Quote

"You are not your thoughts, but you are the thinker of your thoughts." – *Unknown*

Insight

Defusion helps create space between you and your thoughts, allowing for greater clarity and perspective in your decision-making.

Task

Practice saying a negative thought in a silly voice or adding "I notice that I'm thinking..." before it. Notice how this changes your emotional response.

Metaphor

The Bubble – Your thoughts are like bubbles; they can float away if you don't hold onto them too tightly.

September 20: Present Moment Awareness

Quote

"The only way to live is by accepting each minute as an unrepeatable miracle." – *Karen Russell*

Insight

Embracing the present as a miracle enhances appreciation for life. Each moment is unique, offering opportunities for joy and connection.

Task

Choose one activity today—eating, walking, or talking—and fully immerse yourself in the experience, noticing every detail.

Metaphor

The Unfolding Flower – Each moment unfolds like a flower, revealing beauty and complexity when observed mindfully.

September 21: Stress

Quote

"You can't stop the waves, but you can learn to surf." – *Jon Kabat-Zinn*

Insight

Managing stress is about learning to ride the waves rather than trying to stop them. Adaptability is key to resilience.

Task

Write down three ways you've successfully managed stress in the past. Reflect on how you can apply these strategies now.

Metaphor

The Sailboat – Stress is like the wind for a sailboat; you can't control it, but you can adjust your sails to navigate through it.

September 22: Anger

Quote

"The greatest remedy for anger is delay." – *Seneca*

Insight

Taking time before reacting can prevent regrettable actions. Delaying your response allows for a more measured and thoughtful reaction.

Task

When feeling anger today, pause for a few moments before responding. Use this time to reflect on your feelings and possible responses.

Metaphor

The Pressure Cooker – Anger builds like pressure in a cooker; releasing it gradually can prevent an explosion.

September 23: Apathy

Quote

"In the middle of difficulty lies opportunity." – *Albert Einstein*

Insight

Apathy can mask opportunities for growth. Shifting your perspective can reveal potential in challenging situations.

Task

Reflect on a recent experience where you felt apathetic. Write down any potential opportunities that could arise from that situation.

Metaphor

The Diamond in the Rough – Apathy may hide the diamond; it takes time and effort to uncover its brilliance.

September 24: Committed Action

Quote

"It does not matter how slowly you go as long as you do not stop." – *Confucius*

Insight

Progress is about consistency rather than speed. Taking small, committed actions can lead to significant changes over time.

Task

Commit to a daily habit for the next week that aligns with your values. It could be as simple as a daily walk or journaling.

Metaphor

The Marathon Runner – Every step you take in the race of life contributes to your journey; pace yourself for lasting success.

September 25: Values

Quote

"Happiness is when what you think, what you say, and what you do are in harmony." – *Mahatma Gandhi*

Insight

Aligning your thoughts, words, and actions with your values creates a sense of inner peace and fulfillment.

Task

Reflect on how you can better align your daily actions with your core values. Make one change today to bridge that gap.

Metaphor

The Tapestry – Your life is a tapestry woven with the threads of your values; each action adds to the beauty of the whole.

September 26: Acceptance

Quote

"The first step toward change is awareness. The second step is acceptance." – *Nathaniel Branden*

Insight

Awareness and acceptance are foundational for personal growth. Recognising your current state is essential for making meaningful changes.

Task

Practice mindful breathing for five minutes. Focus on accepting your thoughts and feelings as they are, without judgement.

Metaphor

The Open Door – Acceptance is like an open door; it welcomes all experiences, allowing you to step into new possibilities.

September 27: Defusion

Quote

"Thoughts are not facts." – *Unknown*

Insight

Recognising that thoughts do not define you fosters resilience and flexibility. You can choose how to respond to them.

Task

Write down a thought you often believe is true. Now, challenge its validity by listing evidence against it.

Metaphor

The Theatre – Your mind is like a theatre; you can choose which thoughts to focus on and which to ignore.

September 28: Present Moment Awareness

Quote

"The mind is like water. When it's turbulent, it's difficult to see. When it's calm, everything becomes clear." – *Prasad Mahes*

Insight

Calmness allows for clarity and perspective. Practising mindfulness can help settle your mind and enhance awareness.

Task

Spend ten minutes in silence today, observing your thoughts without judgement. Just notice what arises.

Metaphor

The Calm Lake – A calm lake reflects the world beautifully; a clear mind reflects clarity in life's decisions.

September 29: Stress

Quote

"Stress is caused by being 'here' but wanting to be 'there.'" – *Eckhart Tolle*

Insight

Being present in the moment can alleviate stress. Acceptance of your current situation is a powerful tool for peace.

Task

List three aspects of your current situation that you can accept today, recognising that acceptance can lead to greater peace.

Metaphor

The Heavy Cloud – Stress is like a cloud that blocks the sun; acceptance allows the light to shine through again.

September 30: Apathy

Quote

"The only way to do great work is to love what you do." – *Steve Jobs*

Insight

Reigniting your passion can combat apathy. Engaging with what you love can rejuvenate your spirit.

Task

Think of an activity you enjoy. Spend time doing it today, fully immersing yourself in the experience.

Metaphor

The Spark – Your passion is a spark; fan it into a flame to illuminate your path and dispel the shadows of apathy

OCTOBER

October 1: Committed Action

Quote

"The journey of a thousand miles begins with one step."
– *Lao Tzu*

Insight

Taking that first step towards your goals is crucial. Every small action contributes to significant progress over time.

Task

Identify a goal you've been putting off. Write down the first step you will take to move towards it and do it today.

Metaphor

The Seedling – Just as a seedling grows into a mighty tree with nurturing, your small actions cultivate your dreams into reality.

October 2: Values

Quote

"Your values create your actions, and your actions create your life." – *Unknown*

Insight

Understanding your core values helps you make choices aligned with what truly matters to you, creating a fulfilling life.

Task

Write down your top three values. Reflect on how your actions this week have aligned with these values.

Metaphor

The Compass – Your values are like a compass, guiding you toward your true north, ensuring you stay on course.

October 3: Acceptance

Quote

"Acceptance is the key to all our problems." – *Unknown*

Insight

Acceptance opens the door to change. By acknowledging your current reality, you create the space needed for growth.

Task

Identify something in your life that you've been resisting. Practice acceptance by writing a letter to yourself acknowledging this situation.

Metaphor

The Open Hand – Acceptance is like an open hand; it allows experiences to flow in and out without clenching tightly.

October 4: Defusion

Quote

"Don't believe everything you think." – *Unknown*

Insight

Defusion techniques help create distance from your thoughts, allowing you to observe them without judgement.

Task

When a negative thought arises today, write it down. Then, add "I am having the thought that..." before it to create distance.

Metaphor

The Cloud – Your thoughts are like clouds; they come and go, but you can choose to observe them rather than get caught in the storm.

October 5: Present Moment Awareness

Quote

"Realize deeply that the present moment is all you have." – *Eckhart Tolle*

Insight

Practicing present moment awareness enriches your experiences and enhances your appreciation of life's beauty.

Task

Spend five minutes today focusing on your breath. Notice each inhale and exhale without distraction.

Metaphor

The Stopwatch – Life is measured in moments; being present allows you to fully experience each tick of the clock.

October 6: Stress

Quote

"Stress is not what happens to us. It's our response to what happens. And response is something we can choose." – *Viktor E. Frankl*

Insight

Your response to stress can be managed. Choosing how to react empowers you and can significantly reduce stress levels.

Task

Today, when faced with stress, pause and take three deep breaths before responding. Observe the difference it makes.

Metaphor

The Umbrella – Stress is like rain; while you can't control the weather, you can choose to use an umbrella to protect yourself.

October 7: Anger

Quote

"Anger is a wind which blows out the lamp of the mind."
– *Robert Green Ingersoll*

Insight

Anger can cloud your judgement. Recognising it allows you to address it constructively rather than reactively.

Task

When you feel anger rising today, take a moment to identify the underlying emotion driving it. Write it down.

Metaphor

The Fog – Anger can be like fog, obscuring your vision; take a moment to clear your mind and find clarity.

October 8: Apathy

Quote

"If you're not living on the edge, you're taking up too much space." – *Anonymous*

Insight

Apathy can hinder your potential. Engaging with life more fully can help you rediscover passion and purpose.

Task

Try something new today—whether it's a hobby, a food, or an activity. Notice how this impacts your feelings of engagement.

Metaphor

The Dormant Volcano – Underneath apathy lies potential; when you ignite that spark, you unleash your inner strength.

October 9: Committed Action

Quote

"Success is the sum of small efforts, repeated day in and day out." – *Robert Collier*

Insight

Success builds on consistency. Committing to small, manageable actions leads to substantial achievements over time.

Task

Set a daily goal for the week and track your progress. Celebrate each small achievement along the way.

Metaphor

The Mountain Climber – Each step taken is a victory on your journey to the summit; persistence is key to reaching the top.

October 10: Values

Quote

"In the end, we will remember not the words of our enemies, but the silence of our friends." – *Martin Luther King Jr.*

Insight

Acting according to your values fosters deeper connections. Standing by your beliefs can inspire others and enrich your relationships.

Task

Reach out to a friend or family member today to show support. Reflect on how this aligns with your values of connection and kindness.

Metaphor

The Bridge – Your values are bridges that connect you to others; they create pathways for understanding and support.

October 11: Acceptance

Quote

"The greatest discovery of my generation is that a human being can alter his life by altering his attitudes."
– *William James*

Insight

Acceptance of your thoughts and feelings can alter your experience. Shifting your perspective creates opportunities for change.

Task

Today, practice accepting your feelings without trying to change them. Notice how this impacts your overall mood.

Metaphor

The Garden – Acceptance is like tending to a garden; nurturing it allows for growth and flourishing despite weeds.

October 12: Defusion

Quote

"Thoughts are like clouds; they come and go." – *Unknown*

Insight

Defusion helps you observe thoughts without attachment. This practice fosters mental clarity and emotional resilience.

Task

When a distressing thought arises today, visualise it as a cloud drifting away. Allow it to pass without judgement.

Metaphor

The Train – Your thoughts are like trains passing by; you don't have to board every one of them.

October 13: Acceptance

Quote

"Acceptance doesn't mean resignation; it means understanding that something is what it is and that there's got to be a way through it." – *Michael J. Fox*

Insight

Acceptance is the first step toward change. Embracing your reality enables you to find constructive paths forward.

Task

Reflect on a situation in your life that you've been resisting. Write down how acceptance could change your perspective on it.

Metaphor

The Open Door – Acceptance is like an open door; it allows you to step into new possibilities rather than staying stuck in discomfort.

October 14: Stress

Quote

"It's not stress that kills us; it is our reaction to it." – *Hans Selye*

Insight

Your reaction to stressors is within your control. Recognising this empowers you to choose healthier responses.

Task

Identify a current stressor and write down three alternative ways to respond to it that could reduce its impact on your life.

Metaphor

The Weather – Stress is like the weather; while you can't control it, you can prepare and adapt to it.

October 15: Anger

Quote

"For every minute you remain angry, you give up sixty seconds of peace of mind." – *Ralph Waldo Emerson*

Insight

Anger often distracts you from the peace that is available in the present moment. Letting go of anger can restore your inner calm.

Task

When you feel anger today, pause and take three deep breaths. Reflect on what you truly want in that moment instead of reacting.

Metaphor

The Storm – Anger is like a storm cloud; it may overshadow your day, but with time, the sun will shine again if you allow it.

October 16: Apathy

Quote

"The opposite of love is not hate; it's indifference." – *Elie Wiesel*

Insight

Apathy can sap your energy and joy. Engaging with your passions can reignite your enthusiasm for life.

Task

Identify an area of your life where you feel apathetic. Take one small step today to reconnect with your interest in that area.

Metaphor

The Dimming Light – Apathy is like a light dimming; take action to turn it back on and illuminate your path.

October 17: Committed Action

Quote

"What lies behind us and what lies before us are tiny matters compared to what lies within us." – *Ralph Waldo Emerson*

Insight

Your internal strength fuels your actions. Drawing on this can help you pursue your goals with determination.

Task

Reflect on a challenge you've overcome. Write down what strengths you drew on and how they can support you in future actions.

Metaphor

The Well – Your inner resources are like a well; drawing from it allows you to nourish your journey.

October 18: Values

Quote

"Live your values, not your fears." – *Unknown*

Insight

Focusing on your values helps you make decisions that lead to a fulfilling life, reducing fear-driven choices.

Task

Today, make one decision based on your values rather than fear. Reflect on how this feels and the impact it has on your day.

Metaphor

The Lighthouse – Your values are like a lighthouse, guiding you safely through the storms of fear and uncertainty.

October 19: Acceptance

Quote

"The first step toward change is awareness. The second step is acceptance." – *Nathaniel Branden*

Insight

Awareness of your thoughts and feelings is crucial for change. Acceptance is the bridge to transformation.

Task

Spend a few moments today reflecting on an aspect of your life that you struggle to accept. Write about how acceptance might change your perspective.

Metaphor

The River – Acceptance is like a river; it flows around obstacles, finding its way despite challenges.

October 20: Defusion

Quote

"You are not your thoughts." – *Unknown*

Insight

Defusion allows you to see thoughts as separate from your identity, reducing their power over you.

Task

Today, whenever a negative thought arises, remind yourself, "This is just a thought." Observe it without judgement.

Metaphor

The Balloon – Your thoughts are like balloons; you can let them float away without holding onto them.

October 21: Present Moment Awareness

Quote

"Each morning we are born again. What we do today matters most." – *Buddha*

Insight

Focusing on the present enriches your experiences and helps you appreciate the beauty in everyday moments.

Task

Take a walk today and consciously notice your surroundings. What do you see, hear, and feel? Write down your observations.

Metaphor

The Photographer – Life is a series of snapshots; being present allows you to capture each moment beautifully.

October 22: Stress

Quote

"Stress is like a rocking chair; it gives you something to do but gets you nowhere." – *Glenn Turner*

Insight

Understanding that stress can be unproductive allows you to shift your focus to more effective coping strategies.

Task

Identify a stressor today and write down two productive steps you can take to address it rather than letting it consume you.

Metaphor

The Burden – Stress is a heavy load; learn to lighten it by sharing your burdens with others or seeking solutions.

October 23: Anger

Quote

"Anger is never without a reason, but seldom with a good one." – *Benjamin Rush*

Insight

Recognising the underlying reasons for anger helps you address the root causes rather than merely reacting to the symptoms.

Task

Reflect on a recent moment of anger. Write down what triggered it and what underlying feelings contributed to your reaction.

Metaphor

The Volcano – Anger can build pressure like a volcano; understanding its source can help you prevent an eruption.

October 24: Apathy

Quote

"To be yourself in a world that is constantly trying to make you something else is the greatest accomplishment." – *Ralph Waldo Emerson*

Insight

Reconnecting with your authentic self can combat apathy. Embracing who you are can reignite your passions.

Task

Spend time today doing something that reminds you of your true self, whether it's a hobby, interest, or spending time with loved ones.

Metaphor

The Phoenix – Just as the phoenix rises from its ashes, rediscover your passions and let them reignite your spirit.

October 25: Committed Action

Quote

"Do what you can, with what you have, where you are." – *Theodore Roosevelt*

Insight

Taking action, even in small ways, empowers you to create change and achieve your goals despite your circumstances.

Task

Identify one small action you can take today that aligns with your long-term goals. Follow through and reflect on the experience.

Metaphor

The Path – Your actions pave the way; even the smallest step can lead you to your destination.

October 26: Values

Quote

"Value is not what you get. It's what you give." – *Unknown*

Insight

Aligning your actions with your values not only enhances your life but positively impacts those around you.

Task

Today, look for opportunities to give back or support others in a way that aligns with your values.

Metaphor

The Tree – Just as a tree provides shade and shelter, living your values creates a supportive environment for others.

October 27: Acceptance

Quote

"Everything can be taken from a man but one thing: the last of the human freedoms – to choose one's attitude in any given set of circumstances." – *Viktor Frankl*

Insight

Acceptance gives you the freedom to choose how to respond to life's challenges rather than being a victim of circumstances.

Task

Choose one challenge in your life. Write down how acceptance of this situation might change your emotional response.

Metaphor

The Anchor – Acceptance anchors you in turbulent waters, providing stability and clarity.

October 28: Defusion

Quote

"You can't stop the waves, but you can learn to surf." – *Jon Kabat-Zinn*

Insight

Defusion allows you to surf the waves of thought without being overwhelmed, helping you maintain balance amidst turmoil.

Task

Practice a defusion technique today when a negative thought arises. Observe it without attachment, letting it pass by.

Metaphor

The Surfboard – Defusion is your surfboard; it helps you navigate the waves of your thoughts skillfully.

October 29: Present Moment Awareness

Quote

"The only thing we have to fear is fear itself." – *Franklin D. Roosevelt*

Insight

Focusing on the present can alleviate fear by reducing the power of thoughts about the past or future.

Task

Take a few moments to breathe deeply and centre yourself. Focus on the sensations in your body and your immediate surroundings.

Metaphor

The Compass – Present moment awareness is your compass, helping you navigate your path without being lost in past or future worries.

October 30: Stress

Quote

"It's not the load that breaks you down, it's the way you carry it." – *Lou Holtz*

Insight

Understanding how you manage stress can help you carry your burdens more effectively and maintain balance in life.

Task

Reflect on your current stress management techniques. Identify one that is effective and one that may need adjustment.

Metaphor

The Backpack – Your stress management skills are like a backpack; how you pack and carry your load makes all the difference.

October 31: Anger

Quote

"Holding onto anger is like drinking poison and expecting the other person to die." – *Buddha*

Insight

Letting go of anger not only frees you from its hold but also opens the door to healthier relationships.

Task

Identify someone you've held anger toward. Write a letter expressing your feelings, but don't send it. Reflect on the release you feel.

Metaphor

The Stone – Anger is like a stone in your pocket; carrying it weighs you down. Let it go to lighten your load.

NOVEMBER

November 1: Values

Quote

"Your values are your compass. They guide you through the challenges of life." – *Unknown*

Insight

Clarifying your values helps you make choices aligned with what truly matters to you.

Task

Spend a few minutes writing down your top five values. Reflect on how these values influence your daily decisions.

Metaphor

The North Star – Your values are like the North Star; they provide direction and help you navigate through life's uncertainties.

November 2: Committed Action

Quote

"Action may not always bring success, but there is no success without action." – *Benjamin Disraeli*

Insight

Taking committed action towards your goals, despite fear or uncertainty, is essential for growth and fulfilment.

Task

Identify one small action you can take today that aligns with your values and goals. Commit to doing it.

Metaphor

The Bridge – Committed action is like a bridge; it connects where you are to where you want to be.

November 3: Acceptance

Quote

"The greatest weapon against stress is our ability to choose one thought over another." – *William James*

Insight

Acceptance involves recognising and choosing how to respond to our thoughts and feelings, rather than avoiding or resisting them.

Task

Practice accepting a thought or feeling today without trying to change it. Notice how that changes your experience.

Metaphor

The Balloon – Acceptance is like letting go of a balloon; once you release it, it can float freely without your grip.

November 4: Present Moment Awareness

Quote

"Wherever you are, be all there." – *Jim Elliot*

Insight

Being fully present enhances your experience of life and helps you connect with your surroundings and emotions.

Task

Take a few minutes to engage your senses. Notice three things you can see, hear, and feel right now.

Metaphor

The Garden – Present moment awareness is like tending to a garden; it flourishes when you nurture it with your attention.

November 5: Anger

Quote

"Anger is a wind that blows out the lamp of the mind." – *Robert Green Ingersoll*

Insight

Recognising the impact of anger can help you manage it constructively, allowing for clarity and calmness.

Task

Reflect on a recent situation that made you angry. Consider how you could respond differently next time.

Metaphor

The Fog – Anger can be like fog; it obscures your vision. Finding clarity helps you navigate through it.

November 6: ADHD

Quote

"You can't use up creativity. The more you use, the more you have." – *Maya Angelou*

Insight

Embracing your creativity can be a strength when living with ADHD, allowing for unique problem-solving approaches.

Task

Engage in a creative activity today, whether it's drawing, writing, or brainstorming. Let your ideas flow without judgement.

Metaphor

The Firefly – Your creativity is like a firefly; it lights up the darkness and guides you when you embrace it.

November 7: Committed Action

Quote

"Success is the sum of small efforts, repeated day in and day out." – *Robert Collier*

Insight

Consistent small actions lead to significant changes over time. Commit to your goals with daily efforts.

Task

Set a specific daily goal for the next week that aligns with your values. Track your progress and celebrate small wins.

Metaphor

The Mosaic – Each small action is like a piece of a mosaic; together, they create a beautiful picture of your life.

November 8: Acceptance

Quote

"Sometimes the most productive thing you can do is relax." – *Mark Black*

Insight

Acceptance can lead to relaxation and increased productivity by reducing resistance to your current situation.

Task

Schedule a time today to relax and simply be. Engage in a calming activity without distractions.

Metaphor

The River – Acceptance is like a river; it flows smoothly when you let go of rocks that create obstacles.

November 9: Values

Quote

"In the end, you're not judged by your intentions; you're judged by your actions." – *Unknown*

Insight

Your values should be reflected in your actions. Aligning them can create a fulfilling and meaningful life.

Task

Identify one action you can take today that aligns with your core values and commit to it.

Metaphor

The Roadmap – Your values act as a roadmap, guiding you toward the destination of your meaningful life.

November 10: Present Moment Awareness

Quote

"The mind is like water. When it's turbulent, it's difficult to see. But when it's calm, everything becomes clear." – *Prasad Mahes*

Insight

Calming your mind through present moment awareness can provide clarity in decision-making and daily activities.

Task

Practice a mindfulness exercise today, focusing on your breath for five minutes. Notice the clarity that arises.

Metaphor

The Mirror – Present moment awareness is like a clear mirror; it reflects your true self when the mind is calm.

November 11: Anger

Quote

"The best fighter is never angry." – *Lao Tzu*

Insight

Remaining calm and composed allows you to address issues without the cloud of anger hindering your judgement.

Task

When you feel anger today, pause and ask yourself what you truly need in that moment instead of reacting immediately.

Metaphor

The Ocean – Anger can be like turbulent seas; finding your calm allows you to navigate through life's challenges.

November 12: ADHD

Quote

"The difference between successful people and others is how long they spend time feeling sorry for themselves."
– *Barbara Corcoran*

Insight

Focusing on solutions rather than setbacks is vital for growth and success, especially for those with ADHD.

Task

Identify a challenge you face and brainstorm three possible solutions or coping strategies to address it.

Metaphor

The Ladder – Overcoming challenges is like climbing a ladder; each step brings you closer to your goals.

November 13: Committed Action

Quote

"Do not wait to strike till the iron is hot, but make it hot by striking." – *William Butler Yeats*

Insight

Taking initiative is key to achieving your goals. Committed action creates opportunities.

Task

Identify a project or goal you've been putting off and take the first step today to move it forward.

Metaphor

The Engine – Committed action is the engine that drives your dreams into reality.

November 14: Self-as-Context

Quote

"You are not what you think. You are the awareness that observes your thoughts." – *Eckhart Tolle*

Insight

Recognising yourself as the observer of your thoughts allows for greater flexibility in how you respond to them.

Task

Take a few moments today to observe your thoughts without judgement. Notice how this perspective changes your experience.

Metaphor

The Sky – Your thoughts are like clouds passing through the sky; they come and go, but the sky remains constant.

November 15: Values

Quote

"Act as if what you do makes a difference. It does." – *William James*

Insight

Your actions, guided by your values, have a significant impact on both yourself and the world around you.

Task

Choose one value and find a way to express it today, whether through an act of kindness or a commitment to yourself.

Metaphor

The Seed – Your values are like seeds; when nurtured, they grow into actions that can flourish in the world.

November 16: Present Moment Awareness

Quote

"The present moment is filled with joy and happiness. If you are attentive, you will see it." – *Thich Nhat Hanh*

Insight

Being fully aware of the present can enhance your appreciation for life, fostering joy and contentment.

Task

Set a timer for five minutes today and focus on your breath. Notice the sensations and thoughts that arise without judgement.

Metaphor

The Clock – The present moment is like a clock; it ticks away the seconds of life that we often overlook.

November 17: Anger

Quote

"Anger is a feeling that makes your mouth work faster than your mind." – *Unknown*

Insight

Recognising the impulsiveness of anger allows for better control over reactions, leading to more thoughtful responses.

Task

When anger arises today, take a moment to breathe before responding. Reflect on what you truly want to convey.

Metaphor

The Fire – Anger is like a fire; it can either warm or destroy, depending on how you manage it.

November 18: ADHD

Quote

"It's not about having the time. It's about making the time." – *Unknown*

Insight

Managing ADHD effectively requires proactive planning and prioritisation to create the time you need for tasks.

Task

Plan your day today with specific time slots for tasks you've been postponing. Stick to the schedule as best as you can.

Metaphor

The Juggler – Managing ADHD is like juggling; it takes practice to keep everything in the air without dropping a ball.

November 19: Committed Action

Quote

"Success is walking from failure to failure with no loss of enthusiasm." – *Winston S. Churchill*

Insight

Every step you take, even in failure, is part of your journey toward success. Maintaining enthusiasm is crucial.

Task

Think of a recent setback. Identify one lesson learned and commit to applying it moving forward.

Metaphor

The Climber – Committed action is like climbing a mountain; each step forward brings you closer to the summit, regardless of the obstacles.

November 20: Acceptance

Quote

"Acceptance is the first step to change." – *Unknown*

Insight

Embracing acceptance opens the door to change, allowing you to move forward rather than stay stuck in resistance.

Task

Identify something in your life you're resisting. Write down how accepting it might change your perspective.

Metaphor

The Key – Acceptance is like a key; it unlocks the door to new possibilities and paths.

November 21: Values

Quote

"To live is the rarest thing in the world. Most people exist, that is all." – *Oscar Wilde*

Insight

Living in alignment with your values is essential for a fulfilling life, turning mere existence into meaningful living.

Task

Reflect on your life. Are your daily actions reflecting your core values? Choose one action today to better align them.

Metaphor

The Lighthouse – Your values act like a lighthouse, guiding you safely through the stormy seas of life.

November 22: Present Moment Awareness

Quote

"The past is a ghost, the future a dream, and all we ever have is now." – *Buddha*

Insight

Focusing on the now helps you connect with reality and enjoy the richness of your experiences.

Task

Take a mindful walk today. Pay attention to your surroundings and the sensations of each step you take.

Metaphor

The Window – Present moment awareness is like looking out a window; it allows you to see what's happening outside in real-time.

November 23: Anger

Quote

"For every minute you remain angry, you give up sixty seconds of peace of mind." – *Ralph Waldo Emerson*

Insight

Letting go of anger restores your peace of mind, allowing for a more serene existence.

Task

Reflect on what anger costs you. Write down three benefits of letting go of that anger.

Metaphor

The Weight – Anger is like carrying a heavy weight; when you let it go, you feel light and free.

November 24: ADHD

Quote

"ADHD is not a deficit of attention, but a deficit of attention to the right things." – *Unknown*

Insight

Focusing your attention on what truly matters is essential for harnessing the strengths of ADHD.

Task

Identify the top three priorities in your life. Write them down and plan how to focus your attention on these today.

Metaphor

The Spotlight – Your attention is like a spotlight; directing it toward what matters illuminates your path forward.

November 25: Committed Action

Quote

"The future depends on what you do today." – *Mahatma Gandhi*

Insight

Every action you take today shapes your future. Small, consistent actions build the foundation for your dreams.

Task

Identify a goal and break it down into actionable steps. Choose one step to take today.

Metaphor

The Building Blocks – Committed actions are like building blocks; each one adds strength to your foundation.

November 26: Acceptance

Quote

"When you accept what is, you are free to make what could be." – *Unknown*

Insight

Acceptance allows for creativity and new possibilities to emerge, paving the way for change.

Task

Think of an aspect of your life that you resist. Practice accepting it for the day and notice how that shifts your perspective.

Metaphor

The Blanket – Acceptance wraps around you like a warm blanket, providing comfort amidst discomfort.

November 27: Values

Quote

"Your values are your own. They are your true north." – *Unknown*

Insight

Identifying and living your values leads to authenticity and fulfilment in life.

Task

Reflect on a recent decision. Did it align with your values? Write about the experience and how you can align future decisions.

Metaphor

The Anchor – Your values are like an anchor; they hold you steady during the storms of life.

November 28: Present Moment Awareness

Quote

"Today is the only day. Yesterday is gone." –*John Wooden*

Insight

Embracing the present empowers you to live fully rather than be trapped in past regrets or future anxieties.

Task

Practice being fully present in your next conversation. Listen attentively and engage with the moment.

Metaphor

The Canvas – The present moment is like a blank canvas; what will you create with your focus today?

November 29: Anger

Quote

"Anger is a choice." – *Unknown*

Insight

Recognising that you have a choice in how to respond to anger can empower you to choose peace instead.

Task

In a situation that frustrates you, pause and choose your response thoughtfully. Write about the outcome.

Metaphor

The Switch – Your response to anger is like a switch; you can choose to turn it on or off at any moment.

November 30: ADHD

Quote

"Focus on the journey, not the destination." – *Greg Anderson*

Insight

Emphasising the process over the outcome can help reduce pressure and enhance enjoyment, especially when managing ADHD.

Task

Choose one task to complete today and immerse yourself fully in the process rather than worrying about the result.

Metaphor

The Journey – Life is a journey; enjoying the ride is just as important as reaching your destination.

November 31: Reflection and Integration

Quote

"The journey of a thousand miles begins with one step."
– *Lao Tzu*

Insight

Each small step you take towards understanding and implementing ACT principles contributes to your overall growth.

Task

Reflect on the past month. What have you learned about yourself? Write down three insights that you will carry into next month.

Metaphor

The Tapestry – Your experiences weave together like a tapestry, each thread representing a lesson that enriches your life.

DECEMBER

December 1: Acceptance

Quote

"Acceptance of what has happened is the first step to overcoming the consequences of any misfortune." – *William James*

Insight

Embracing acceptance allows you to move forward rather than being anchored to the past.

Task

Identify a recent event you've resisted. Write down how accepting it might change your feelings about it.

Metaphor

The River – Acceptance is like a river flowing past obstacles; it finds a way around rather than being stuck.

December 2: Values

Quote

"What you do makes a difference, and you have to decide what kind of difference you want to make." – *Jane Goodall*

Insight

Your values guide your actions, shaping the difference you make in the world.

Task

List your top three values. Choose one to focus on this week and plan an action that aligns with it.

Metaphor

The Compass – Your values serve as a compass, guiding your decisions and actions in the right direction.

December 3: Present Moment Awareness

Quote

"The only moment that matters is the present moment."
– *Unknown*

Insight

Focusing on the present enhances your ability to appreciate life as it unfolds.

Task

Spend five minutes today simply observing your surroundings. What do you see, hear, and feel?

Metaphor

The Spotlight – Present moment awareness is like a spotlight, illuminating what truly matters right now.

December 4: Anger

Quote

"Holding onto anger is like drinking poison and expecting the other person to die." – *Buddha*

Insight

Letting go of anger frees you from its grip and restores your inner peace.

Task

Write down one anger you're holding onto. List the steps you can take to let go of it.

Metaphor

The Anchor – Anger can weigh you down like an anchor; releasing it allows you to sail freely.

December 5: Committed Action

Quote

"The price of inaction is far greater than the cost of making a mistake." – *Meister Eckhart*

Insight

Taking action, even imperfectly, leads to growth and learning.

Task

Identify a small action you've been postponing and commit to completing it today.

Metaphor

The Footsteps – Each committed action is like a footprint on your path; they lead you forward, step by step.

December 6: ADHD

Quote

"ADHD is not a disorder, it's a different order." – *Unknown*

Insight

Embracing your unique way of thinking can unlock creativity and innovation.

Task

Today, try a task in a new way that reflects your creative thinking style.

Metaphor

The Kaleidoscope – Your mind is like a kaleidoscope, creating beautiful patterns when you embrace its uniqueness.

December 7: Self-as-Context

Quote

"You are not your thoughts; you are the observer of your thoughts." – *Unknown*

Insight

Separating your identity from your thoughts empowers you to choose your responses.

Task

Spend a few minutes observing your thoughts without judgement. Notice how this perspective shifts your experience.

Metaphor

The Mountain – Your thoughts are like clouds over a mountain; the mountain remains unaffected by the changing weather.

December 8: Values

Quote

"The things you own end up owning you." – *Fight Club by Chuck Palahniuk*

Insight

Your values should drive your choices, not material possessions or external pressures.

Task

Reflect on a purchase you regret. What value did it conflict with? Write about how to align future decisions with your values.

Metaphor

The Sail – Your values are like sails on a boat; they catch the wind and guide you in the right direction.

December 9: Present Moment Awareness

Quote

"Be where you are; otherwise, you will miss your life." – *Buddha*

Insight

Fully experiencing the present moment enriches your life and creates lasting memories.

Task

Practice mindfulness during a mundane activity today, such as eating or washing dishes. Focus on the sensations involved.

Metaphor

The Camera – Present moment awareness is like adjusting your camera focus; it helps you see the beauty in the details.

December 10: Anger

Quote

"Anger is a natural response; it's how you handle it that makes the difference." – *Unknown*

Insight

Understanding the root of your anger can help you address it more constructively.

Task

Think about a recent situation that made you angry. Write down what triggered that anger and how you can respond differently next time.

Metaphor

The Volcano – Anger is like a volcano; if not managed, it can erupt. Learning to channel it can lead to constructive outcomes.

December 11: Committed Action

Quote

"Success is the sum of small efforts, repeated day in and day out." – *Robert Collier*

Insight

Consistency in your actions, no matter how small, leads to significant progress over time.

Task

Choose a habit you want to develop. Set a specific time each day this week to practice it.

Metaphor

The Garden – Committed actions are like tending a garden; with consistent care, it flourishes and bears fruit.

December 12: ADHD

Quote

"ADHD is a different way of thinking, not a flaw." – *Unknown*

Insight

Embracing your unique cognitive style can lead to innovative solutions and creativity.

Task

Find a creative solution to a problem you're facing today. Let your mind wander and explore unconventional ideas.

Metaphor

The Puzzle – Your mind is like a puzzle; it may be challenging, but when the pieces fit together, the picture is beautiful.

December 13: Self-as-Context

Quote

"You are the author of your own story." – *Unknown*

Insight

Recognising yourself as the storyteller empowers you to reshape your narrative.

Task

Write a short paragraph describing a challenging moment in your life. Now, rewrite it from a perspective of growth and resilience.

Metaphor

The Pen – You hold the pen of your life; every day is a blank page where you can write a new story.

December 14: Acceptance

Quote

"Acceptance doesn't mean resignation; it means understanding that something is what it is and that there's got to be a way through it." – *Michael J. Fox*

Insight

Acceptance allows you to acknowledge your feelings without judgement, paving the way for healing and growth.

Task

Identify a situation in your life that you are resisting. Write down how accepting this situation could change your perspective.

Metaphor

The River – Acceptance is like a river flowing around obstacles, finding its way instead of fighting against the current.

December 15: Present Moment Awareness

Quote

"The present moment is filled with joy and happiness. If you are attentive, you will see it." – *Thich Nhat Hanh*

Insight

Being present allows you to fully experience the joy in life, enhancing your overall well-being.

Task

Practice gratitude today by writing down three things you appreciate about the present moment.

Metaphor

The Gift – Each moment is a gift; unwrap it with presence and mindfulness to reveal its treasures.

December 16: Anger

Quote

"Anger can be a gift if you learn to listen to it." – *Unknown*

Insight

Anger can signal unmet needs or boundaries that require attention; listen to its message.

Task

Identify an unmet need that triggers your anger. Write about how you can address this need constructively.

Metaphor

The Alarm – Anger is like an alarm; it alerts you to something important that needs your attention.

December 17: Committed Action

Quote

"The future depends on what you do today." – *Mahatma Gandhi*

Insight

Taking consistent action today sets the foundation for your future achievements.

Task

Write down a goal you want to achieve. List three specific actions you can take this week to work towards it.

Metaphor

The Steps – Each committed action is like a step on a staircase, leading you closer to your goal.

December 18: ADHD

Quote

"ADHD is not about the inability to pay attention; it's about the ability to pay attention to many things at once." – *Unknown*

Insight

Your ability to multitask can be an asset when harnessed appropriately.

Task

Choose a task that requires focus and set a timer for 25 minutes. Allow yourself to work intently during that time.

Metaphor

The Juggler – Your mind is like a juggler, capable of keeping multiple balls in the air with practice and focus.

December 19: Self-as-Context

Quote

"You are not defined by your mistakes; you are defined by how you rise after falling." – *Unknown*

Insight

Viewing yourself as separate from your mistakes enables you to learn and grow from them.

Task

Reflect on a past mistake. Write about what you learned from it and how it has contributed to your growth.

Metaphor

The Phoenix – Like a phoenix rising from the ashes, you can transform mistakes into valuable lessons.

December 20: Values

Quote

"Live your values; every day is a choice." – *Unknown*

Insight

Consistently aligning your actions with your values cultivates a more fulfilling life.

Task

Take a moment to identify a value you want to embody today. Choose one specific action to express it.

Metaphor

The Flame – Your values are like a flame, guiding your way and illuminating your path.

December 21: Present Moment Awareness

Quote

"Wherever you are, be all there." – *Jim Elliot*

Insight

Being fully present enhances your engagement and satisfaction in life.

Task

Practice being present in your interactions today. Put away distractions and focus fully on the person you're with.

Metaphor

The Lighthouse – Present moment awareness is like a lighthouse, guiding your attention and illuminating your experiences.

December 22: Anger

Quote

"Anger is a valid emotion, but it must be expressed wisely." – *Unknown*

Insight

Channelling anger into constructive actions can lead to positive change.

Task

Identify a situation that angers you. Write down one action you can take to address the underlying issue constructively.

Metaphor

The Fire – Anger is like fire; it can either destroy or provide warmth, depending on how you manage it.

December 23: Committed Action

Quote

"Action is the foundational key to all success." – *Pablo Picasso*

Insight

Taking action, regardless of the outcome, is essential for growth and progress.

Task

Set a small, achievable goal for today. Complete it, and take note of how it feels to accomplish something.

Metaphor

The Builder – Each action is a brick; together, they create the structure of your dreams.

December 24: ADHD

Quote

"Your attention is a treasure; spend it wisely." – *Unknown*

Insight

Managing your focus can enhance productivity and satisfaction in your daily tasks.

Task

Identify a distraction that often pulls your attention away. Set boundaries around it today to maintain focus.

Metaphor

The Treasure Map – Your attention is like a treasure map; where you choose to focus determines your destination.

December 25: Self-as-Context

Quote

"The more you know yourself, the more you forgive yourself." – *Maxime Lagace*

Insight

Understanding yourself fosters self-compassion and acceptance of your imperfections.

Task

Write a letter to yourself filled with kindness and understanding. What do you wish to forgive?

Metaphor

The Mirror – Knowing yourself is like looking in a mirror; it reflects both strengths and vulnerabilities.

December 26: Values

Quote

"Value your values. Live your values." – *Unknown*

Insight

Your values shape your identity and influence your choices every day.

Task

Choose one value that's important to you and plan a small action to express it today.

Metaphor

The Guiding Star – Your values are like stars in the night sky, guiding you through the darkness.

December 27: Present Moment Awareness

Quote

"Mindfulness isn't difficult, we just need to remember to do it." – *Sharon Salzberg*

Insight

Practising mindfulness can ground you in the present, enhancing clarity and calm.

Task

Set a timer for five minutes and focus on your breath. Notice the sensations of each inhale and exhale.

Metaphor

The Anchor – Mindfulness is your anchor, keeping you steady amidst the storms of life.

December 28: Anger

Quote

"To be angry is to let others' mistakes punish yourself." – *Unknown*

Insight

Releasing anger allows you to reclaim your power and peace of mind.

Task

Take a moment to reflect on what triggers your anger. How can you let go of its hold on you today?

Metaphor

The Balloon – Letting go of anger is like releasing a balloon; it floats away, freeing you from its weight.

December 29: Committed Action

Quote

"Commitment is the foundation of great accomplishments." – *Heidi Reeder*

Insight

Your commitment to your goals propels you towards success and fulfilment.

Task

Identify a long-term goal. Write down three short-term actions you can take to move closer to it.

Metaphor

The Ladder – Each committed action is a rung on the ladder, helping you reach new heights.

December 30: Values

Quote

"Your values define who you are; they are the compass that guides you." – *Unknown*

Insight

Reflecting on your values helps you make decisions that align with your true self and aspirations.

Task

Identify a value that has been important to you this year. Write about how you can continue to embody it in the upcoming year.

Metaphor

The Compass – Your values are like a compass, guiding you through the choices and challenges of life.

December 31: Committed Action

Quote

"What you do today can improve all your tomorrows." – *Ralph Marston*

Insight

Ending the year with intentional action sets a positive tone for the year ahead.

Task

Reflect on your accomplishments this year. Write down one action you can take today that will contribute to your goals for the next year.

Metaphor

The Seed – Every committed action is like planting a seed; with care and time, it will grow into something beautiful.

CONDITIONS AND STRUGGLES

Addiction

Addiction is a complex condition, a brain disorder that is manifested by compulsive substance use despite harmful consequences. It affects the brain's reward system and leads to long-term changes in brain function.

1. **Key Features:** Compulsive behaviour
2. Loss of control
3. Craving for substances
4. **ACT Approach:** Acceptance strategies can help individuals acknowledge their cravings without acting on them, while committed actions can guide them toward healthier choices and a values-driven life.

Addiction is often viewed through a pathological lens, leading to shame and stigma. However, ACT understands that behaviours associated with addiction are attempts to cope with underlying pain or discomfort. Individuals may engage in substance use as a means of escaping emotional distress or seeking connection. Symptoms can include compulsive behaviour, cravings, and withdrawal symptoms.

ACT encourages individuals to observe their cravings and the context in which they arise, fostering a non-judgmental acceptance of their experience. By identifying personal values, individuals can work towards meaningful goals that replace maladaptive behaviours. For example, someone who uses alcohol to cope with social anxiety may learn to engage in activities that align with their values of social connection, even while experiencing discomfort.

ADHD (Attention-Deficit/Hyperactivity Disorder)

ADHD is a neurodevelopmental disorder characterised by patterns of inattention, hyperactivity, and impulsivity that can interfere with functioning or development. It often persists into adulthood, impacting various areas of life.

1. **Key Features:** Difficulties with focus and organisation
2. Impulsivity
3. Hyperactivity
4. **ACT Approach:** The principles of mindfulness in ACT can enhance present moment awareness, helping individuals with ADHD become more attuned to their thoughts and feelings, thus reducing impulsivity and enhancing self-regulation.

ADHD is often characterised by inattention, hyperactivity, and impulsivity. These traits can lead to behaviours that distract individuals from their values, such as focusing on immediate gratification rather than long-term goals. Symptoms can include difficulty concentrating, forgetfulness, and impulsive decisions.

Rather than pathologising these traits, ACT encourages individuals with ADHD to harness their unique cognitive styles. By focusing on present moment awareness, individuals can improve their attention and reduce impulsivity. For example, a person with ADHD might use mindfulness techniques to stay engaged during a task, thereby aligning their actions with their value of achievement.

Anxiety

Anxiety is a common mental health condition marked by excessive worry, fear, or apprehension. It can manifest in various forms, such as Generalised Anxiety Disorder (GAD), panic disorder, or social anxiety disorder.

1. **Key Features:** Persistent worry
2. Physical symptoms (e.g., increased heart rate, sweating)
3. Avoidance of anxiety-provoking situations
4. **ACT Approach:** ACT techniques promote acceptance of anxious thoughts and feelings, encouraging individuals to engage in committed actions aligned with their values despite experiencing anxiety.

Anxiety often manifests as excessive worry, fear, or avoidance of situations that trigger discomfort. These behaviours can lead individuals away from their values of connection, growth, and exploration. Symptoms may include restlessness, racing thoughts, physical symptoms like a rapid heartbeat, and avoidance behaviours.

ACT teaches individuals to accept their anxious thoughts and feelings rather than fighting against them. This acceptance fosters a sense of psychological flexibility, enabling individuals to engage in valued actions despite their anxiety. For instance, a person who experiences social anxiety may choose to attend a gathering, acknowledging their fear but prioritising their value of connection with friends.

Apathy

Apathy is a state of indifference or lack of interest in engaging with life or activities that were once enjoyable. It can be a symptom of various mental health conditions, including depression.

1. **Key Features:** Lack of motivation
2. Disinterest in activities
3. Emotional numbness
4. **ACT Approach:** ACT helps individuals reconnect with their values and intrinsic motivations, fostering committed actions that can rekindle interest and engagement in life.

Apathy is characterised by a lack of motivation or interest in activities that were once enjoyable, often linked to depression. This condition can lead to withdrawal from social connections and avoidance of responsibilities, steering individuals away from their values of engagement and joy. Symptoms may include emotional numbness, disinterest, and fatigue.

In ACT, apathy is understood not as a failure but as a disconnection from values. By gently encouraging individuals to reconnect with their core values and explore small, manageable steps towards engagement, ACT promotes movement towards a more fulfilling life. For instance, an individual who feels apathetic about work might rediscover their passion for their career by identifying projects that resonate with their values.

Anger

Anger is a natural emotional response to perceived threats or injustices. However, when it becomes chronic or uncontrollable, it can lead to significant interpersonal and emotional issues.

1. **Key Features:** Intense feelings of displeasure or hostility
2. Physical reactions (e.g., increased heart rate, muscle tension)
3. Impulsive behaviours in response to anger
4. **ACT Approach:** ACT encourages acceptance of anger without judgment, allowing individuals to explore the underlying values and triggers associated with their anger and take constructive actions in response.

Anger is often labelled as a negative emotion, but it can serve as a signal indicating that something is wrong or unjust. However, when anger becomes chronic, it can lead to destructive behaviours that push individuals away from their values, such as connection and compassion. Symptoms of anger may include irritability, a tendency to lash out, physical tension, and aggressive behaviour.

From an ACT perspective, anger is neither good nor bad; it is a natural response that can provide insight into personal boundaries and values. By learning to accept and acknowledge anger without judgment, individuals can explore the underlying values that their anger points to. For instance, if someone feels angry about a social injustice, they can channel that anger into committed actions that promote change, thus moving closer to their values of fairness and integrity.

Stress

Stress is the body's response to demands or pressures, which can be positive or negative. Chronic stress can lead to serious health problems and affect emotional well-being.

1. **Key Features:** Physical symptoms (e.g., headaches, fatigue)
2. Emotional symptoms (e.g., irritability, anxiety)
3. Behavioural changes (e.g., withdrawal, changes in eating habits)
4. **ACT Approach:** Mindfulness practices in ACT help individuals remain present during stressful situations, promoting acceptance and reducing avoidance behaviours that can exacerbate stress.

Stress is a response to perceived challenges or threats and can manifest physically and emotionally. Chronic stress can result in avoidance behaviours, irritability, and emotional fatigue, pushing individuals away from their values of well-being and balance. Symptoms include headaches, fatigue, anxiety, and sleep disturbances.

ACCEPTANCE AND COMMITMENT THERAPY (ACT)

Acceptance

Acceptance involves acknowledging and embracing unpleasant thoughts, feelings, and sensations instead of attempting to avoid or suppress them. This process helps individuals reduce their struggle with negative experiences and enhances emotional resilience.

Example: In the metaphor of *The River*, the flowing river represents acceptance of life's challenges. Just as the river navigates around rocks and bends without resisting its course, individuals can learn to accept their feelings, allowing them to move forward in life.

Cognitive Defusion

Cognitive defusion is the practice of distancing oneself from unhelpful thoughts and beliefs. This process helps individuals observe their thoughts as mere words or pictures in their minds rather than as truths that dictate their actions.

Example: The metaphor of *The Balloon* illustrates cognitive defusion, where holding onto a balloon represents clinging to negative thoughts. Releasing the balloon can signify letting go of those thoughts, allowing individuals to see them as transient rather than as integral parts of their identity.

Present Moment Awareness

Present moment awareness encourages individuals to focus on the here and now rather than ruminating about the past or worrying about the future. This component promotes mindfulness, enabling a richer experience of life.

Example: The *Lighthouse* metaphor serves to illustrate present moment awareness, where the lighthouse provides clarity in a foggy environment, similar to how mindfulness helps individuals remain grounded and focused amidst life's distractions.

Self-as-Context

Self-as-context refers to the understanding that one's self is not defined solely by thoughts or feelings but rather as an observer of those experiences. This perspective allows individuals to separate themselves from their thoughts, promoting self-acceptance and reducing self-criticism.

Example: The metaphor of *The Phoenix* highlights self-as-context, illustrating how individuals can rise from adversity. Recognising that challenges are part of their journey allows them to redefine their identities through resilience and growth.

Values

Values are the guiding principles that shape an individual's life decisions and actions. Identifying and clarifying values helps individuals pursue meaningful goals, providing direction in their lives.

Example: In the metaphor of *The Compass*, values are likened to a compass that provides direction. Just as a compass points to true north, identifying personal values guides decision-making and helps individuals stay on a meaningful path in life.

Committed Action

Committed action involves taking steps towards living in alignment with one's values, even in the presence of difficult thoughts and feelings. This commitment to action encourages individuals to move forward in life and strive for their goals.

Example: The *Builder* metaphor emphasises committed action, where each brick laid represents a step taken towards building a fulfilling life. Just as a builder focuses on constructing a solid structure, individuals can commit to actions that reflect their values, leading to personal growth and success.

ACKNOWLEDGEMENT

First and foremost, I would like to extend my deepest gratitude to my wife, Janet. Your unwavering support, love, and encouragement have been my foundation throughout this journey. Thank you for being by my side through every challenge and triumph.

To all the incredible therapists and fellow professionals I've had the privilege of working with over the years, your dedication and passion for helping others inspire me daily. Special thanks to all the individuals in recovery from addiction and alcoholism who have shared their stories with me and allowed me to walk alongside them on their journeys. Your resilience and determination continue to be a source of learning and motivation.

This book would not exist without the profound contributions of the pioneers of Acceptance and Commitment Therapy (ACT). I want to express my heartfelt thanks to Dr. Steven C. Hayes, the founder of ACT, whose innovative work has transformed the lives of so many. Your dedication to developing ACT and advancing contextual behavioural science has created a powerful, compassionate framework for change.

I am also deeply grateful to Russ Harris, whose clear, accessible teachings have made ACT understandable and practical for therapists and individuals alike. Your work has had an enormous impact on the ACT community and beyond.

Additionally, I would like to acknowledge the work of so many others who have shaped the field of ACT and contributed to the development of contextual behavioural science, including but not limited to:

- Dr. Kelly G. Wilson
- Dr. Kirk Strosahl
- Dr. Patricia J. Robinson
- Dr. Robyn Walser
- Dr. John Forsyth
- Dr. JoAnne Dahl
- Dr. Mark Webster
- Dr. Louise Hayes
- Dr. Emily Sandoz
- Dr. Ian Stewart
- Dr. Jason Luoma

Thank you to the wider contextual science community, who continue to push the boundaries of our understanding of human suffering and thriving. Your research, dedication, and insights are integral to the continued growth of ACT and its effectiveness in helping people live richer, more meaningful lives.

Lastly, I want to express my gratitude to every person who reads this book and takes the courageous step to integrate ACT into their daily life. May it serve as a tool to help you navigate your struggles and discover your own path to a rich and meaningful existence.

ABOUT THE AUTHOR

Bill Stevens

Bill Stevens entered active recovery from substance and alcohol abuse in 1995. Over the years, he has faced many of the struggles that accompany addiction, including anxiety, anger, ADHD, apathy, and stress. These experiences fuelled his desire to help others find freedom from addiction and lead a rich, meaningful life. Since then, Bill has dedicated his career to working as a specialist addiction therapist, initially training and gaining valuable experience with The Priory Group and later establishing his own private practice. He has helped countless individuals, families, and groups discover paths out of addiction and into healthier, value-driven lives.

In 2012, Bill was introduced to Acceptance and Commitment Therapy (ACT), immediately recognising its pragmatic and flexible approach, particularly for individuals with addiction. ACT resonated deeply with Bill's therapeutic philosophy, focusing on helping people become "unstuck" from their struggles and rediscovering the freedom to live a fulfilling life. His extensive clinical experience has shown that those who benefit the most from therapy often develop a daily habit of mindful practice and values-based action.

Through his work, Bill saw the need for a daily tool that complements ACT therapy — one that can be used every morning to foster psychological flexibility and strengthen a person's commitment to living in accordance with their values. This inspired him to compile ACT Today, a daily companion for those undergoing therapy or striving to implement ACT principles into their lives. Bill believes that this one-day-at-a-time approach helps clients manage their struggles more effectively by breaking the overwhelming process of change into manageable, daily steps.

Bill is the co-founder of RedChair Addiction Specialists, based in Manchester, which operates across the UK and Europe. Since 1998, Bill has provided bespoke addiction treatment and case management, supporting clients in overcoming a wide range of behavioural and substance addictions. He combines his expertise in Cognitive Behavioural Therapy (CBT), Transactional Analysis (TA), and Rogerian therapy with his passion for ACT, offering a unique, integrative approach to therapy.

As the only Certified Intervention Professional (CIP) in the UK until 2021, Bill has maintained rigorous ethical standards, ensuring his clients receive the highest level of care. In addition to his work as a psychotherapist, Bill has supported the mental and emotional well-being of sports teams, such as Wolverhampton Wanderers Football Club, and he has appeared as a regular expert on the BBC, discussing addiction, family interventions, and broader societal issues around substance abuse.

Bill continues to advocate for quality addiction care, offering training to other professionals and working within television production to support actors facing emotionally demanding roles. He remains committed to helping individuals overcome addiction and thrive in recovery, using ACT principles to guide them on the path to a rich and meaningful life.

Printed in Great Britain
by Amazon

48889821R00228